ACCESS YOUR ONLINE RESOURCES

Supporting Children and Young People with Test Anxiety in School is accompanied by a number of printable online materials, designed to ensure this resource best supports your professional needs.

Go to https://resourcecentre.routledge.com/speechmark and click on the cover of this book.

Answer the question prompt using your copy of the book to gain access to the online content.

SUPPORTING CHILDREN AND YOUNG PEOPLE WITH TEST ANXIETY IN SCHOOL

This accessible and informative book provides educators with a unique approach to supporting children and young people with test anxiety, combining key research and practical guidance to improve wellbeing and test outcomes.

The book focuses on three core areas for promoting wellbeing: test anxiety theory; 'desirable difficulties'; and self-efficacy theory. Underpinning research is presented in an accessible format and each topic is explored in depth with case studies and reflection points to deepen understanding and bring theory to life. Chapters go on to introduce an innovative, easy-to-implement intervention. The intervention focuses on increasing children's metacognition of their own learning – from how memory works, to knowing how to revise – lowering anxiety around high stakes exams and boosting overall wellbeing and, ultimately, academic success.

Including a wealth of examples and tips for tangibly supporting children and young people's learning outcomes, this book is a crucial read for Special Educational Needs Coordinators (SENCOs), teachers, and anyone with responsibility for the pastoral care and wellbeing of young people.

Helen Barsham has extensive experience working as a head teacher in both primary and secondary settings. She recently completed a Doctorate of Education at the University of Cambridge, which explored pupil wellbeing, metacognition and desirable difficulties, using the 'testing effect' to reduce test anxiety.

SUPPORTING CHILDREN AND YOUNG PEOPLE WITH TEST ANXIETY IN SCHOOL

How to Improve Wellbeing and Give Back Control

Helen Barsham

LONDON AND NEW YORK

Designed cover image: Getty Images

First published 2026
by Routledge
4 Park Square, Milton Park, Abingdon, Oxon OX14 4RN

and by Routledge
605 Third Avenue, New York, NY 10158

Routledge is an imprint of the Taylor & Francis Group, an informa business

© 2026 Helen Barsham

The right of Helen Barsham to be identified as author of this work has been asserted in accordance with sections 77 and 78 of the Copyright, Designs and Patents Act 1988.

All rights reserved. The purchase of this copyright material confers the right on the purchasing institution to photocopy or download pages which bear the support material icon and a copyright line at the bottom of the page. No other parts of this book may be reprinted or reproduced or utilized in any form or by any electronic, mechanical, or other means, now known or hereafter invented, including photocopying and recording, or in any information storage or retrieval system, without permission in writing from the publishers.

Trademark notice: Product or corporate names may be trademarks or registered trademarks, and are used only for identification and explanation without intent to infringe.

British Library Cataloguing-in-Publication Data
A catalogue record for this book is available from the British Library

ISBN: 978-1-032-87711-2 (hbk)
ISBN: 978-1-032-87707-5 (pbk)
ISBN: 978-1-003-53406-8 (ebk)

DOI: 10.4324/9781003534068

Typeset in Interstate
by Deanta Global Publishing Services, Chennai, India

Access the Support Material: https://resourcecentre.routledge.com/speechmark

For Mum

CONTENTS

Acknowledgments   x
Preface   xi
Introduction   xii
Chapter Overviews/Takeaway Resources   xiv

1 **What is Test Anxiety?**   1

2 **Fear appeals**   22

3 **Using Desirable Difficulties to Give Back Control**   33

4 **Self-efficacy in Test-Taking**   58

5 **Intervening in Test Anxiety**   71

6 **The Intervention: Giving Back Control – Reducing Test Anxiety – How To Do It**   80

7 **Learning and Metacognition**   115

8 **The Dream for Education: On the Soapbox**   125

9 **School Development Plan to Give Students Back Control for Taking Exams**   138

10 **In Conclusion**   142

Appendix A   145
Appendix B   147
Index   148

ACKNOWLEDGMENTS

I could not have written this book without the Bjorks' wonderful work on 'Desirable Difficulties' (and many other seminal retrieval practice authors, referenced throughout).

Thanks to Doug Wren and Dave Putwain for always answering my emails so helpfully and their inspirational research, and Doug's permission to share the Children's Test Anxiety questionnaire (see Appendix 1).

I could also not have written this book without the participation of schools, colleagues, parents and, most of all, the students who took part in the research. Big thank you there!

My thanks to my colleagues on the doctoral journey and especially my supervisor Professor Michelle Ellefson at the University of Cambridge.

Last (but not least), my thanks to my family and friends – especially Mike, Anna, Mimi, Pluto, Rusty and Harry who were all part of this journey.

PREFACE

In writing this book, I have made it as easy as possible for those of you with busy days, in educational settings, to implement the changes suggested here. This is because I know how precious time is, in education. There never seems to be enough of it. But there is a need for this change. I wanted this to be a 'hands on', 'here you go' approach to helping students with test anxiety. I hope to have provided a book with some theory but, importantly, a book in which there are resources that you are able to 'pick up and run with'.

As an educator for twenty-nine years at the time of writing, I understand the pressures on the various systems in schools. Many suggestions in this book, are just that – ideas that you may be able to use in your specific setting. I am not trying to teach 'granny to suck eggs' at any point and offer this book with due humility to the vast amount of knowledge, experience and love you all have for 'the kids' out there. Feel free to adopt, adapt to your setting but attribute credit where credit is due ...

I completed my doctorate so that I could help students **tangibly** through managing the complex and huge problem that is test anxiety, so I hope you will find this book is a **tangible** resource.

The Interim Curriculum Review has just been published (March 2025). The authors suggest that the primary sector is working. This book is for **primary, secondary and beyond**. However, we're missing a chance here! **Learning how to learn, learning for life** could really happen if you took exams away. Year 6 students are often taught for the Standard Assessment Tests (SATs) exams. You only have to look at the Key Stage 2 and 3 dip literature (how students don't progress when they move to secondary school) to see how the 'blocked' or learned knowledge for tests can drop off over the summer break. It's more than just a length-of-the-holiday problem. It's because Year 6 learning is learning for exams. The awe and wonder of the early years firmly behind them. By the time students get to secondary education, learning habits are harder to break. It makes sense to get primary students into great learning habits rather than not using massed or blocked practice (which is what teaching to exams does). Currently, I believe there is so much 'blocked learning', aided and abetted by General Certificate of Secondary Education (GCSE) requirements that we're missing an opportunity to revolutionise how students learn for life rather than for exams.

Educators, there is also a separate 'user-friendly' guide called 'Manage Test Anxiety' for your students, by Triggerhub publishing, available by searching online.

Teachers/Parents/Anyone who is interested – just email me: helen@fighttestanxiety.com

Web: fighttestanxiety.com

INTRODUCTION

I have long been concerned with the pressures of high stakes tests on young people. I am not a fan of the current UK system of examinations but have taken many students through this system in both state and independent schools and, not least, navigated my own children through the system.

The problem of feeling anxious about tests, **test anxiety**, is a huge one.

In this book, I look at test anxiety and explain how an intervention using the theories of **self-efficacy** (belief in capability) and **'desirable difficulties'** can be used to reduce test anxiety. I cover the problem of test anxiety and supply the intervention, which is now packaged as a Scheme of Work, and is easily deliverable in schools and colleges. There are three practical resources for rolling out the management of test anxiety in educational settings:

1. The intervention, now cleverly disguised as a possible Personal, Social, Health and Economic (PSHE), or PASTORAL, Scheme of Work, deliverable to all ages in schools (from 9 years to 18 and beyond) **with all the resources**. This does not have to be PSHE/PASTORAL lesson or time but this work seems to fit in neatly in this category or however your setting can work it. **Its aim is to reduce anxiety around exams through creating excellent revision habits**. (See Chapter 6.)
2. A suggestion for a strand of a **School Development Plan** aimed at embedding optimal practice around managing tests. It's no good just delivering a unit of work (in this case it's also an intervention) as a standalone measure. Changes in the way we approach testing in schools and colleges needs to be from the roots up! (See Chapter 9.)
3. A programme for Teacher Training on Desirable Difficulties. (See Chapter 8.)

However, before you skip ahead and access the 'hands on' resources, I think you will get more out of them if you can possibly take the time to read these first few chapters. I know time is precious but an understanding of what test anxiety is and how it is exacerbated by 'fear appeals' is important. Equally so, the information on using cognitive science 'desirable difficulties' to manage test anxiety thereby increasing self-efficacy in test taking. Chances are, you will find useful points that you can apply to other aspects of your roles as educators in these chapters too.

Furthermore, I encourage you, as educators, to take a look at **how feedback around tests is managed in your setting**. This is important.

Occasionally, I step onto a mini-soapbox with my beliefs about the current test-taking regimes in the education system in the UK. I hope I have kept my '**soapbox**' focus to just this theme and fairly minimal. I signpost when I am about to step on it!

The **golden thread** of the book is understanding how we need to **give control back** to the students who are anxious about taking tests and how we can do this in an educational setting. The theories of **test anxiety**, **retrieval practice (in this book retrieval practice with a difference – see NB)** as it is **not** used for subject content recall (as per the teaching standards) but **recall of a wellbeing strategy** and **self-efficacy theory** are explained. I argue that by understanding how the brain learns and particularly how memory works for tests, we can give students back 'control'.

Throughout, I have often used the words **school**, **college** and **educational setting**. If you don't belong in one of these categories, it does not mean that the information in this book is not relevant to you. Testing and anxiety and anxiety about testing can happen at any stage of life and in any career (think driving tests), so it may well be that learning how memory works is useful in giving confidence outside of the educational context. I have also used the words **high-stakes tests**, and **tests** and **exams** interchangeably and to mean more or less the same thing – important evaluative assessments that have *a lot* riding on them in terms of outcomes.

NB: I want to make one point very clearly, hence placing it here. Although the intervention (Scheme of Work) shared with you in this book (see Chapter 6) uses the principles of retrieval practice or the testing effect, I used retrieval practice to recall positive thinking: **your testing routes are well-oiled** and **study, test, test, test** is best. There is a great volume of research 'out there' dedicated to retrieval practice of content needed for tests. Great! I have drawn on this research but 'tweaked' the principle to create a pastoral intervention. I applied the tenets of retrieval practice or recall to a wellbeing strategy to create a mantra for students who are anxious about taking tests. **This book is about retrieval practice for wellbeing** and about finding solutions to help give control back to students in the often nerve-wracking situations of exams.

At the beginning of each chapter is a summary of what is covered and some key terms. At the end of the chapter, I have isolated some 'takeaways' and set you some (optional) retrieval practice homework! In addition, where possible I have given some realistic scenarios so that you can apply what you have read to the issue. These might be useful for Continuing Professional Development (CPD). In doing this, the information in this book is elaborated and cued into your memory more easily! I have also put important summaries into **In a Nutshell** boxes and, when I need to drive home a point, I use a **Nitty Gritty** box.

So: feel free to ignore the '**soapbox'**; use the **Nutshells** for key information to remember; and keep in mind that **Nitty Gritty** is important for the students (and the world!). At the end of Chapters 1 to 5 I also include a **memory hotspot**, just a little extra information about memory for fun!

CHAPTER OVERVIEWS/ TAKEAWAY RESOURCES

These provide a summary of chapter content followed by the key terms used in the chapters. (A key term appears in bold the first time it is included in the chapter text itself.) In Chapters 4, 6, 8 and 9 plus Appendix A and Appendix B, you will also find resources that you can reproduce for your students to complete or for your own use.

Chapter 1: What is Test Anxiety? is an overview of test anxiety and the issue of giving students back control in testing situations. I have suggested some practical preliminary steps in **changing a culture** where 'tests' are in control rather than students and teachers! *An initial parent engagement event is suggested and wording suggested.*

Chapter 2: Fear Appeals discusses the research into **'Fear Appeals'**, what they are and how to avoid and use them. It all requires a close look at your own everyday practice.

Chapter 3: Using Desirable Difficulties to Give Back Control is a long chapter as we get to the real recipe for reducing test anxiety through revision skills. I go into **'retrieval practice'** and the wider brush of **'desirable difficulties'**; knowledge biases are touched upon, as are **metacognition of learning** and the important issue of **feedback**. *Metacognition of learning resource and optimal testing/revision schedule.*

Chapter 4: Self-efficacy in Test Taking delves briefly into **self-efficacy theory** and the **golden thread** again of how we can give students back control.

Chapter 5: Intervening in Test Anxiety is a preliminary to the intervention itself and explains why writing tasks feature in the intervention and some other 'bits and pieces' that I wasn't sure where to place in this book.

Chapter 6: Intervention: Giving Back Control – Reducing Test Anxiety – How To Do It is the **intervention**, the *Schemes of Work* for all age groups and the accompanying resources. Grab it and go!

Chapter 7: Learning and Metacognition focuses on the problem of blocked practice, metacognition and judgements of learning.

Chapter 8: The Dream for Education: On the Soapbox is where I let my hair down for a bit and discuss my dream for education. *Chunks of text for a PowerPoint for training teachers/parents on 'Desirable Difficulties' are included.*

Chapter 9: School Development Plan to Give Students Back Control for Taking Exams is what it is.

Chapter 10: In Conclusion is where I leave you!

1 What is Test Anxiety?

> **What to Expect**
>
> This chapter includes a brief history of test anxiety and how test anxiety can affect students. It explains that we need to give back control to the students. The chapter includes how to find out which students are high in test anxiety by conducting research in the classroom; using questionnaires; and how to involve parents and train teachers around the subject of test anxiety. The initial parent event that is needed is covered.

> **Key Terms**
>
> **desirable difficulties:** interleaving, spacing, the testing effect, moving room to room
> **fear appeals:** see Chapter 2, but basically when someone scares you about exams by reminding you of the possible consequences
> **intervention:** what we do/did to increase control, reduce worry and manage test anxiety
> **perceived control:** how much control a student feels they have over the exam
> **self-efficacy:** belief in capability
> **self-knowledge beliefs:** in this context, how a student rates their ability to takes tests
> **state and trait anxiety:** state from current context, trait more likely inherited.
> **test anxiety:** feeling anxious about taking tests
> **transactional:** how students draw in anxiety from test-taking situations
> **worry/worrying:** a cognitive process

We live in an evaluative society. Students must take high stakes tests to access options in life: from SATs (Statutory Assessment Tests) in the UK in Year 6 (10–11-year-olds) to GCSEs (General Certificate in Education) at 16 years of age that determine 16–18-year-olds' education paths, and then A levels or other pathways at 18 years old that may determine

DOI: 10.4324/9781003534068-1

university entrance. In independent schools, scholarship papers are taken aged 11 or 13 years to determine, scholarship status, which may result in fee reductions or access to some free tuition.

All of these high stakes tests listed can cause anxiety in some students (and their teachers, peers and parents).

In the years since the lockdowns (a result of the global pandemic in 2020-2021), schools have struggled increasingly to get some students to attend school. These students still have the same high stakes tests to take at the end of various key stages of learning. (These stages are: KS2 up to 11 years; KS3 up to 14 years; KS4 up to 16 years; and KS5 up to 18 years.)

KS2 students may sit SATs or other senior school entrance exams and scholarships. KS4 generally covers GCSEs or BTech exams, and KS5 is predominantly A levels, some International Baccalaureate (IB) and a plethora of medical, veterinary, Oxbridge and other tests for university entry.

The topic of increase in anxiety levels for the school age group, especially teenagers, is rarely out of the news. Yet, schools do not have specific programmes for managing **test anxiety**. Aiming to give students more control over their feelings about taking high stakes tests should be explicitly taught as part of the PSHE/Pastoral curriculum in schools and colleges. Teaching students how to learn so that they can control their test anxiety is kind, helpful and useful. The **intervention** (see the PSHE/Pastoral Scheme of Work in Chapter 6) is for *all* students, not just test-anxious ones – all students' wellbeing can benefit.

A Brief History of Test Anxiety

When I began to research test anxiety, I did not realize what a vast topic I was stepping into. As you may expect, there is a huge array of psychological theories that have underpinned and evolved behind test anxiety theory: attentional, motivational, expectancy and arousal theories (Zeidner, 1998). Concepts include 'evaluation anxiety', 'negative self-beliefs' and 'skills deficits' (Zeidner and Matthews, 2005). There are different 'models' of test anxiety and different constructs. Where does test anxiety come from? Is it a cognitive, physiological or behavioural problem or a mixture? Can test anxiety be good for you?

The first thing I did in my research was to identify the model or construct of test anxiety that I felt could reasonably apply to most of the students I knew who were anxious about taking tests. I mainly concentrated on cognitive test anxiety, commonly known as **worrying** about exams. And I focused on **self-knowledge beliefs**, which may include: feelings of not being able to 'do' the exams; not being able to pass the exams; a lack of belief in ability to be able to get through the exams. Fear of failure! Zeidner and Matthews (2005) model of 'self-referent executive function' is my 'go to' test anxiety construct as detailed in Figure 1.1. My plan of attack to reduce feelings of worry, give back control and reduce test anxiety was focused on the self-knowledge beliefs box.

Some students are naturally more anxious than others. This is a result of proximal (near) and distal (more distant) factors (Zeidner, 1998). Zeidner (2014) highlights the school environment as a major proximal factor. For example, this can be the physical context of

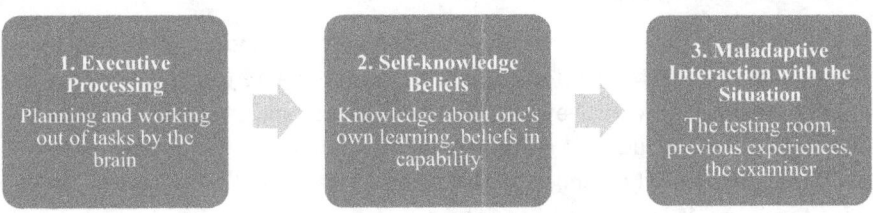

Figure 1.1 The S-REF Model – Self-Referent Executive Function (Zeidner and Matthews, 2005).

an examination setting, but also the result of many peer and social pressures – not least teacher, parental, and peer pressure that can be conveyed in **fear appeals** (see Chapter 2) (e.g. Putwain and Best, 2011; Putwain, et al., 2016a,b). Proximal anxiety relates to the status quo, the context and what may be anxiety-producing at the time, the **state** of the person. Distal anxiety is related to relatives, family, a genetic inheritance. There may be a history of anxiety in the family, or some issue of childhood trauma or other circumstances that have led to anxiety. It may exist some way back in the past either through an event or genetically, but it is a trait in the person. Some students will have **trait anxiety** that leads to state anxiety and some students may have state anxiety brought on just by the thought of exams themselves.

Spielberger and Vagg (1995) suggested that there is 'a state' test anxiety and 'a trait' test anxiety. This means there are some people who are naturally more anxious than others and, when placed in an anxiety inducing situation such as an exam, this 'state' anxiety can tip them over the edge. However, there are some individuals who are not usually anxious but for whom the state of taking an exam makes them anxious. It's the idea of the surroundings, the context, all adding to the anxiety.

Importantly, in any given classroom at any time, there will be at least 10-20% of students who feel anxious about taking tests (Cizek and Borg, 2010; Putwain and Daly, 2014). It is important that this statistic is acknowledged, and provision made for these students. In doing so, it is conceivable that a wellbeing strategy around taking tests can be created for all students in education. It is important that this statistic is not just a statistic but motivation for action.

Can test anxiety be good for you? The idea that test anxiety can be facilitative in taking tests is an old one (Alpert and Haber, 1960). It's worth mentioning but important to keep at the forefront of our thinking the chronic and debilitative effects of test anxiety on many students. For some students, a little bit of anxiety before an important exam might help them perform. However, there is a difference between feeling a bit anxious but being 'in the flow' with a test (as described by psychologist Mihaly Csikzentmihalyi in his books and TED Talks) and able to answer the questions and perform, and not being able to perform because of anxiety about the test. Putwain (2020) dismisses the idea of test anxiety being facilitative, **as do I**. I have watched too many students crumble at the thought of exams and seen too many teachers and parents become needlessly stressed to believe that anything good comes from anxiety about tests.

Models of Test Anxiety

A key model of test anxiety was proposed by Liebert and Morris (1967) as being a bi-dimensional construct with worry (cognition) and emotionality (behaviour). This is helpful in identifying **worry** as a cognitive key component of test anxiety separately to behaviour. Some behaviours may include not revising because a student is too anxious or not revising because it's such an overwhelming experience and it's easier to 'fail' and say 'I didn't do any work' than to try and fail because of anxiety.

The wonderfully named Spielberger and Vagg (1995) started the idea of a **transactional** model of test anxiety which, with the idea of **worry**, is the area that my research and resulting intervention, focused on. They define test anxiety as an individual having a tendency to 'worry and intrusive, irrelevant thoughts' (Spielberger et al.,1976).

Zeidner and Matthews (2005) consider multiple factors that lead to test anxiety such as: **negative self-belief**, skills deficits and avoidance motivation. They developed the S-REF (Self-Referent Executive Function) model of test anxiety (see Figure 1.1). This is a transactional model that represents the students as individuals with probable proximal or distal anxiety, drawing additional anxiety from the context they find themselves in such as the preparation or taking of exams, thereby manifesting as trait or state anxiety for the upcoming exam.

Giving Back Control

It is this model of test anxiety (S-REF) that was used as the inspiration for the intervention in my doctoral research that gave students back control in testing situations. It is the idea of being able to control the cognitive process to give back control to the student. The intervention intervenes at Box 2 (see Figure 1.1), the self-knowledge beliefs box, before a student becomes unable to cope with the high stakes test and starts to draw on bad memories or negative thinking. I suggest we could give back control to students by teaching them:

1. how to recognize their knowledge about their own learning, and
2. how memory works, how revising for tests works – actually, in the brain.

If a student knows how memory works, they can tailor their revision process to maximize how their memory is working and draw confidence (self-knowledge beliefs) from knowing that they will be able to recall their revision for tests in a high stakes exam. Just feeling more confident means they can perform better in exams (Bandura, 1997).

Let's recap on Figure 1.1, which appears earlier in this chapter and ask ourselves what's going on here.

What Is Going On Here?

The process starts with executive processing. A student is informed about an exam or a test, or is aware of a test possibly as soon as they enter a given year of learning. They know what the academic implications are. For example, a Y10 student in the UK knows they are starting their GCSE study and that school life becomes very serious from this point onwards (if it wasn't before!) Box 1, Figure 1.1 (Executive Processing) is when a student will start to process what this really means for them. As this process evolves and there's revision schedules and lessons, tutoring happens; there's conversations with friends, parents, teachers and peers. A student who has experienced previous difficulties with tests may start to recall these negative experiences. An anxious student may start to become full of fear. There's feelings of panic, wanting to give up, believing it's easier not to try than try and fail, peer pressure, parent pressure, self-pressure, perfectionism, fear appeals (see Chapter 2); there can be a total lack of self-belief in the ability to take the test. The fear and panic will get in the way of any revision process. If we then add the contextual situation of actual exams where students are parted from their phones (identities?), made to take off watches, use clear plastic water bottles, the deafening silence of an exam room etc., the context can be overwhelming. The rules around taking exams are necessarily stringent but has anyone thought about what these military procedures may do to a student with test anxiety? In schools, there are exam briefings, tutor group briefings, constant reminders, posters put up everywhere: 'SILENCE!' Can you imagine being scared of taking exams? What might all these exam briefings and rules do to a student who is anxious about taking exams? You have a legal obligation with the JCQ (Joint Council for Qualifications), I know, but can you see what all the 'setting up' of exams might do to a test anxious student? We get 'the crumble' or 'the meltdown', the avoidance, the panic, worry, fear, refusal. This is where we need students to draw on the strategies that the intervention (PSHE/Pastoral Scheme of Work) gives them. Well, just before they go into panic mode actually!

My research with the students intervened in Box 2 to try to avoid the contextual 'shove over the cliff edge' of exams that can happen in Box 3, the negative self-spiral of anxiety. My intervention enables anxious students to cope with tests by drawing on positive self-beliefs - **self-efficacy** in test taking. I don't know what to suggest about all the JCQ regulations that have to be followed, but I can imagine how this makes anxious and nervous students feel. The following question is designed to prompt your setting into some creative thinking around the necessary strict rules of administration of exams.

How can you minimize the impact of everything associated with the exam context for test-anxious students? For example, even putting a funny picture on a SILENCE notice can make a positive difference! Would that work? What else could you change to lighten the mood, whilst adhering to official regulations?

The Power Of Contextualization

As a trainee teacher (a long time ago, 1996), I was taught that we must contextualize learning. I remember my early days in a big, comprehensive school in the East End of London, always trying to relate what I was teaching to events and circumstances of the students' lives. As an English teacher, we chose texts with themes that students could relate to: *Chandra*, by Frances Mary Hendry; *Chinese Cinderella*, by Adeline Yen Mar and *The Outsiders*, by S. E. Hinton. We worked hard to engage boys in reading by choosing books that related to their interests. We knew, as teachers, that making learning relatable was key to enjoyable lessons and students being able to grasp concepts, thereby improving outcomes. *Did we ever think of making the process of taking tests relatable? Did we ever contextualize the process?* No, we taught to the exam because that is what we had to do, and we were monitored on our grade successes by the leadership team. (This still happens in schools.) Back in those days, we taught on Saturday mornings too, targeting our D to C grades because we were measured on our A–C grades by the powers that be (and still are!). When I think back, I can see that during the weeks leading up to exams, we were all in a heightened state of being – a 'got to get the best grade' being – carried along on a wave of grade anxiety.

Contextualizing Tests So Students Understand How Memory Works For Tests

Returning to Figure 1.1, Box 2 holds two key ideas for supporting students with test anxiety:

1. knowledge about one's own learning – metacognition of learning; and
2. beliefs in capability.

These two ideas led to the creation of an intervention to support students in managing test anxiety. Knowledge about one's own learning comes from students possessing metacognition about their learning and in the case of exams, metacognition about how their memory works for exams. Do we specifically teach students that in school? How sensible to do so? This led me to the wonderful work of Bjork's **desirable difficulties** (Bjork and Bjork, 2020). Belief in capability falls under the umbrella of self-efficacy theory and the wonderful work of Albert Bandura (1997). I thought if I can 'nail' Box 2 and prevent Box 3 from happening, it will provide the students who have test anxiety with a strategy that supports them.

I was also able to draw on the excellent research of David Putwain and his colleagues. Putwain and Aveyard (2018) discuss the issue of self-belief showing a small to moderate correlation with exam performance. They say that not much research had been done at this stage to look at **how self-belief can act with cognitive test anxiety (or worry)** to predict exam performance. They talk about **control**. How the **perceived control** a student has about taking the exam can affect performance by affecting the worry or cognitive element of test anxiety. Putwain and Symes (2018) suggest that individuals with **high test anxiety** compensate with **more effort** than other students. Interestingly, a student who has trait anxiety and is more naturally anxious may have better coping strategies than someone who has state anxiety and is just anxious about exams. Students with trait anxiety may have developed better anxiety coping mechanisms as a result of being anxious in their lives and are therefore able to transfer coping strategies to test taking contexts.

In a Nutshell

Box 2 in Figure 1.1 holds the key elements of being able to support control by reducing worry by learning about how memory works and therefore altering beliefs about one's ability to take tests.

Box 3 (Figure 1.1) suggests some of what can happen to students who have high test anxiety. The context can be overwhelming, and they can only remember previous negative experiences. As people, we are very good at forgetting the 'good stuff' but can draw relentlessly on bad memories! Test anxious students may get 'brain freeze' as some students have described to me. They have difficulty concentrating and have irrational thoughts. They anticipate failure due to a lack of self-belief. They may have trait anxiety, which is exacerbated in testing situations, or state anxiety, which is a direct result of the exam itself. Or both!

Contextual Exam Anxiety, and State and Trait Anxiety

Many years ago, in an English Language GCSE paper, the writing part of the exam asked students to 'Describe the room you are in'. If you think of an exam room, and for those of you reading this who may have invigilated, it can be an overwhelmingly anxiety-producing experience. I bet the examiners did not consider that there might be test-anxious students, for whom being in the room, let alone writing about it, was totally overwhelming!

As I have mentioned already, the whole exam experience is so different from 'normal' school that it can be totally overwhelming for some students: the lack of sound, the sound of pen on paper, the hushed atmosphere, the no phones (leaving everything a teenager may identify with at the door), plastic water bottles with no labels and the desks, the numbers, the instructions, the rules, the clocks, the strangers – all potentially anxiety inducing. In addition, a student may be recalling a previous negative experience from an exam situation. It's not difficult to understand how overwhelming this situation can be.

How can we expect students to recall the information and content they know when their brain is in fight, flight or freeze modes? Information needs to be in the long-term memory to be able to cope with test anxiety.

There are strategies that schools and colleges can use to help prepare students for these experiences. Most schools these days run 'mock' exams and try to make the experience as near to the real exams as possible. Of course, this is good practice but it's not the only thing that schools could and arguably *should* be doing.

Giving Back Control: First Practical Steps in Schools/Colleges

Nitty Gritty

In giving students back control over taking tests, you will need to **revolutionize** the way you approach tests in your educational setting. As well as an intervention (PSHE/Pastoral scheme – see Chapter 6), you need a whole school/college approach (see Chapter 9).

How do you know if a student has test anxiety? It is usually obvious to a teacher in a classroom. In a busy school day, it's difficult to find the time to have all the conversations you may need to have with individuals, willing them on, trying to give them self-confidence and self-belief. As a teacher, you will try for your subject area, as will a tutor for your tutees, but these can be invariably 'snatched' chats simply due to the demands and pace of a school day. A parents' evening thrown in after mock exams gives precious few minutes to discuss subject-specific strategies (such as, Remember to use PEEL: Point, Evidence, Explanation, Link paragraphs; Check your answers thoroughly; Plan your revision carefully), but at any point, *is the issue of being anxious about tests researched for in your educational setting and an intervention delivered to reduce anxiety levels?*

Chapter 6 of this book sets out what is effectively a PSHE/Pastoral Scheme of Work for you to follow to address the problem of anxiety about taking tests in schools. There is a week-by-week guide and access to all the resources. The hope is that this will help students who are taking tests, but it will not work as effectively as a 'standalone' curriculum delivery unless supported by a whole school strategy about taking tests and how the school approaches this from Day One of a student's life/experience in a school/college. Hence the need for a whole-school approach, known in the trade as a School Development Plan (see Chapter 9).

Who is Anxious About Taking Tests and Preparing the Way?

It is important for an educational setting to know which students are anxious about their upcoming high stakes' tests, which parents are also anxious and which teachers experience stress about exams. I think we are all familiar with terms such as 'helicopter parenting', where the parents are 'circling' the child and the school for the best results. We have heard of 'tiger mums' who have trained their prodigies to jump through numerous academic, social, sporty and musical hoops. I think we all understand the concept of parental expectations and certainly all teachers I worked with wanted students to fulfil their potential. The problems come when parental expectations are way above the potential of the child. This is often a result of a parent being highly successful themselves and assuming their child/children will do the same.

Then there is the issue of perfectionism from the child themselves. So many kids are so hard on themselves these days as social media tells them how wonderful they have to be in every way.

The point of mentioning this is that the first port of call in changing the test taking culture of a school should be in engaging the parents with your pedagogical purpose. As staff will need training in these new concepts, and students will need educating, parents need informing and educating too.

Practical: What to do First

Step 1: Hold a parents' evening

Most of this step will make sense once you have read Chapters 2 and 3 of this book but I have included this here because it is the most sensible first step to take.

Deliver a 'parents' evening' for the Year groups in question four to six months ahead (or thereabouts) of the main test-taking period. In addition, make the content of the parents' evening accessible on video, online, on YouTube – whatever works to get the maximum student and parent engagement in your school. You will explain about using desirable difficulties and fear appeals (outlining a parents' role in both of these – see Chapters 2 and 3) and generally approach the upcoming exams in a different way, explaining that you need parental support.

The evening/online presentation needs to be run by someone who cares about the students' wellbeing. It can be a Pastoral member of staff, a SENCo (Special Educational Needs Coordinator), or a subject teacher. It could be an Early Career Teacher, or anyone really – but it needs to be someone who cares and is interested in this book, and they should ideally be supported in an administrative capacity to pull together the research and in a CPD (continuing professional development) capacity with some time to do the necessary reading – i.e. time to read this book, communicate with stakeholders, run off photocopies (or organize online resources) and tailor these resources/advice to your setting.

In addition to the research, which is largely covered in the content of this book (with references included at the end of every chapter for the enthusiast), you will be talking to a parental audience about keeping a perspective; the dangerous power of peer conversations; fear appeals; and the problem of being an over-anxious parent about exams. (Be careful with this final one, but it does need to be addressed because a parent who is anxious about their child's exams can make the child anxious. It's a sensitive issue; some parents may suffer with anxiety and it may be proximal or distal, hereditary. The main thing is you do have some helpful solutions around exams, and that's the important point to make). You will share the power of the desirable difficulties teaching along with the intervention that the school or college is going to deliver (see details of the PSHE/Pastoral Scheme of Work in Chapter 6). The research will be shared with the parents so that they can understand their role and what they need to say.

This event can be calendarized on a yearly basis.

Suggested Programme Ahead of the Curve

As said, I don't wish to 'do' the proverbial 'granny and eggs' but for those who may find it helpful, I have suggested here some wording and an order for your parent evening/online event that may help. (Also see Chapter 8 for 'PowerPoint chunks' that may be useful or pull your own together from anything in this book.)

The Parent Event (Suggestions)

1. Start the evening by explaining that this evening (whatever and whenever it is) is happening now (four to six months ahead of exams) to avoid any sense of building exam anxiety. It is important to avoid any sense of 'priming' the students, parents and staff, but also important that there is a discussion given young people's anxiety levels.

2. Explain that at least 10–20% of any classroom's students will be anxious about taking exams and that your educational setting is determined to address this problem! You can explain that as teachers, we are always taught to contextualize learning but rarely is the learning for exams explained to students. It makes sense to teach the students how memory works so that they understand the revision processes leading up to exams. By teaching students how memory works we are not just helping their confidence in upcoming exams but teaching them how to learn for life and arguably, in the distant future, they will be equipped to teach their children how to learn.
3. Explain that you have met, as a staff, to discuss the common approaches to teaching exams and have come away from using blanket fear appeals (see Chapter 2) that have been used in the past to motivate lazier students as you recognize that these fear appeals (for example, 'You need to get your Maths and English, otherwise you'll have to re-take them' etc.) can send students who are anxious about exams into meltdown. Explain that you are using the latest research on reducing test anxiety by giving back control to the students through developing their metacognition of the revision process using desirable difficulties (see Chapter 3). In addition, explain that staff are being trained in desirable difficulties too (see Chapters 3 and 8).
4. Explain that in order to deliver the best outcomes, ideally you need to deliver two questionnaires to the students to complete. The data is being used only in school to inform teachers. The intervention/PSHE/Pastoral Scheme of Work will be made available, along with all other PSHE/Pastoral information (wherever you have this type of information available for parents). You might also add a sentence such as: 'Please let us know if you do not wish your child to take part in the questionnaire.' (This isn't necessary, although it's probably courteous. That said, as this data is just for school purposes, make it clear that you will treat it in the same way as you gather other information from the students.) The intervention is 20 minutes per week for six weeks in PSHE/Pastoral lessons.
5. Be prepared for the following.
    - The parent who suggests anxiety can be a good thing before exams. Point them in the direction of David Putwain et al. (2016a,b; 2018a,b).
    - The parents who believe their child benefits from a fear appeal because they know they are lazy.

    You can cover all of this by simply saying that your school is using cutting-edge research (a new approach, the first of its kind in the UK), post-COVID times, to address worries about exams; some students will never reveal they are anxious – even if they are.
6. Next, explain how we are social creatures, and the power of social media and peer groups is second to none through the teen years. If a peer says 'It's too hard, I can't cope, I'm not revising', then this message can be easily absorbed. If only teens could say 'I've studied well because I've tested myself so my testing routes are firing on all cylinders' it would be a much better message.
7. If you have time and know your parents well, it is probably a good idea to invite a discussion about how they manage the run-up to exams at home. What do they say to

their children? However, I'll leave this up to you! You may sense that if the parents lead the conversation, it could go on all evening and it may even encourage disagreement among parents. Explain that we cannot protect our children totally, nor do we wish to encourage the so called 'snowflake' generation, but we must not destroy them either with words like 'If you fail, then it's all over.' Empathize with parents because it's not an easy role at times. Explain that you know it's a difficult middle road to tread as parents, especially if your son/daughter is anxious about tests. That's why it's important that, this evening (or whenever), we are sharing 'the script' with them for the intervention the students will have in school. The power of using desirable difficulties (see Chapter 3). I would also make it very clear that the Scheme of Work will benefit all students' wellbeing whether they are test anxious or not.
8. Deliver the desirable difficulties information. Invite questions. (You'll find chunks for a PowerPoint in Chapter 8, but you may prefer to make your own based on the information in Chapter 3 plus references.)

Step 2: Gauge feelings about exams

Having held a pioneering parent engagement evening in the latest research about managing test anxiety, it's time to gauge students' feelings about exams.

In Step 1, I briefly mentioned two questionnaires to use with students. These are simple and straightforward (as you'll see in the Appendices of this book). I know this because when I started my research I used a different one and all hands in the classroom went up asking: 'What's this, Miss?' So that particular questionnaire was not used. The questionnaires in this chapter have been tried and tested on a range of different-aged students in schools.

There are many problems with using questionnaires but for ease and speed in school and short of swabbing students for cortisol levels (you know how difficult that sort of thing can be in school) questionnaires provide a good snapshot of data that you can work with. Some students will complete them inaccurately, some will mess about with them, but generally most will simply complete them. I used a four-point Likert scale so that answering the questions was not an overwhelming task with too many options. Some students may be absent; this is not a problem either because they can complete it when they can.

It's important to let students know that the data from the questionnaires is confidential and for internal use only; explain it's to 'help us help them'.

The Children's Test Anxiety Questionnaire (Appendix A)

This questionnaire was devised, used and analysed by Wren and Benson in 2004. The reason I chose jt is because it had the input of a teacher and was trialled in schools. It has been used reliably in many subsequent experiments and translated into various languages. It is appropriate for students from aged 9/10 years and upwards. I took out the question 'I check the time' from the original as I think most students are trained to check the time in exams, and so for me it was irrelevant. The questionnaire contains three subscales, which I used for measurement of test anxiety (but you don't really need to know that): Thoughts, Off-Task

Behaviours, and Autonomic Reactions. Essentially, these subscales represent a test anxiety model of cognitive (thoughts) and behaviour (reactions), and the transactional element of test anxiety from the context and surroundings in (off-task behaviours).

Students who answer questions with 3s and 4s on this questionnaire are going to be the students with high test anxiety.

The Confidence Questionnaire (Appendix B)

The second questionnaire is shorter and is aims to look at how confident students feel about taking exams – in other words, how much self-efficacy, belief in capability, they possess. I wrote (and tested) this questionnaire. The questions are reversed in places for my statistical analyses so it's important that the students read them carefully.

Both questionnaires are measured with the same 1, 2, 3, 4-point version of a Likert scale – which I used for this research (and which originated in 1932). I did not want to introduce too many numbers (sometimes scales go up to 10 points), and did not want to use the original 5-point scale, as there is a feeling participants will simply opt for the middle point.

The results for the Confidence questionnaire (Appendix B) need to be looked at carefully: 3s and 4s on the positively worded questions (Q1, Q2, Q3, Q10, Q11, Q12, Q13, Q14, Q15) suggest confidence in test-taking. Conversely, 3s and 4s on Q4, Q5, Q6, Q7, Q8, Q9 suggest a lack of confidence in test-taking. In theory a confident student will score highly on the positively worded questions and will have a low score on the negatively worded questions. A student who is not confident in taking tests will have a low score on the positively worded questions and a high score on the negatively worded questions. It's important to simply ask the students to read the questions carefully and not direct them to the positive or negative language.

Step 3: Study the data

At this point, you need to deliver the questionnaires and their data. In your school or college circumstances, you will not be using this data for research purposes, but it may still be courteous to gain permission. Perhaps you suggested to parents at the parent/online evening to opt in or out of the questionnaires, but you can decide as a school how best to manage this. You are not using the data for research purposes other than internally to help you support the students, so you will do what you usually do when you need to gauge students' opinions. For older students, I would always ask them, directly, for their agreement and explain why we're doing what we're doing. Ultimately, this is meant to be a helpful wellbeing strategy *for all*. Although you are gauging anxiety levels, all students will receive the intervention (PHSE/Pastoral Scheme of Work).

It is sensible and inclusive to deliver the questionnaire to *all* students. This is because you will want to deliver the intervention/PSHE/Pastoral Scheme of Work *to all the students*. Some test anxiety research does just intervene with the students who have the highest test anxiety scores. However, this is often impractical and can be seen as divisive in a school setting. Inclusivity is key.

Moreover, Weems et al. (2009, 2010) suggest using a test anxiety intervention that is administered universally because that may increase general student wellbeing. This may be an unexpected bonus of a test anxiety intervention, and my recommendation is that, for the most part, these questionnaires should be delivered in a 'blanket' fashion to the whole class (unlike fear appeals – which are covered in Chapter 2). By delivering the questionnaires and the intervention/PSHE/Pastoral Scheme of Work in a blanket way, this means that no student or group of students is singled out in the process.

If the questionnaires and intervention are delivered as part of the PSHE/Pastoral curriculum, then parents are usually informed in advance of the topics on the curriculum and thus the questionnaires and content of the intervention can be listed here in whatever form your informing parents about PSHE/Pastoral work in your school takes.

Make sure the students initial the questionnaires so you know who is who. Both questionnaires take about 15-20 minutes in total, together.

What Do You Do With the Data?

Best practice is to share the results of the questionnaires with staff who teach or care for the students. You know your students and you may want to use this data to hold individual conversations, but these would need to be managed carefully. The reason you have delivered the questionnaires a long time ahead of the exams is to avoid the issue of 'priming' or making a student more anxious just before an exam. For some students who have test anxiety, just talking about the questionnaires could make them more anxious. Without being able to judge your individual scenarios, the recommendation is to give the questionnaires out in a blanket way and then share the crucial data or information about who the students with the highest test anxiety are with subject teachers and tutors and key personnel involved with students. It will be important for the SENCo to know this data, as they have responsibility for exam access arrangements. Data could be shared at a staff meeting, Pastoral team discussion, senior leadership meeting, staff briefing – whatever works for the setting you're in.

Problems with Measuring Test Anxiety

It is quite difficult to measure test anxiety. This is because it would be completely distracting to students to try and measure anxiety levels directly before and after an exam. There are one or two experiments that have done this. It might be possible to measure the stress hormone cortisol from a swab. Generally, questionnaires are used but they are not a perfect system. However, they are easily administered in schools/educational settings. The problem with questionnaires, only worth a brief mention here, is that some students may not take the questionnaires seriously thereby skewing the data. Questionnaires can have missing responses and be misread. The good news is that you are not relying on the questionnaires for a measure or seeking statistical significance from them. As a setting you are using them once only, well ahead of an exam to find out more about the students' test anxiety levels and thus, they should be a relatively good system.

What Data Do We Share With Students/Parents?

Parents can request access to this data of course (unless safeguarding is involved in any way). It is probably unhelpful for a school to send the data home though. You may wish to call in specific parents of students who are especially anxious over taking tests if you think they are not aware already. These conversations are probably happening around a child anyway, especially if discussing exam access arrangements for an anxious child. If the data shows a student who is high in test anxiety and who is not considered anxious by the school, this may be worth the SENCo/Pastoral lead/tutor having a conversation with the students, staff and parents. The important thing for a student who is high in test anxiety is that they have the correct access arrangements (which could be a separate room) and/or whatever is tailored to their needs and wishes, and that they are not primed into feeling more anxious about an exam by discussing it. This is why the intervention/PSHE/Pastoral Scheme of Work is delivered in a blanket way so that everyone feels the same and all can benefit. The other important consideration is that you can nurture the test-anxious individual more effectively because you have a new tool at your disposal in the form of the content of this book.

You will know your students and, before you get the results back from the questionnaires, you can probably anticipate them. However, I think this is useful to do to maybe pick up on some students who may not have voiced their anxieties otherwise. Sometimes, this can be the one person you would not expect. It's important to take their answers seriously. The questionnaire may just be the 'out' a person needs; you know the student, intent on seeming and being confident; the one who doesn't care about exams or revising and is especially confident in front of their peers. The swan that is paddling like crazy underneath a cool exterior.

Attributional Training and More Ideas for Supporting Test Anxiety

One suggestion for staff is to have a focus on attributional training in addition to the recommended training on desirable difficulties and fear appeals covered in this book. This could be key to managing test anxiety, especially if you ask the trainer to guide you on managing feedback around tests. This could be done on a one-day INSET (In-Service Training) with an external provider or someone who has the know-how in your setting. This kind of training is designed to increase motivation and encourage achievement by changing how students think about their academic successes and failures so that beliefs will work for them and improve their outcomes. It's about how you manage feedback to students in schools.

How Staff Manage Performance Data and Feedback

How many times do we ask students not to compare their scores on a test with a peer? How much growth mindset (Dweck, 2008) have we done? We say the outcome is not important. What matters are your next steps, and then we get them to DIRT (dedicated improvement or reflection time or, when I first started teaching, direct activities related to texts – they've been around a long time!), or analyse, or do something with a purple or green pen that they are supposed to learn from. We are trained in assessment for learning as teachers but how good at managing feedback to give students control over tests are we? This is an important question because if a setting can nail the feedback, it can add to creating confidence around tests.

In Chapter 3, I will be encouraging you to test your students more, not less. While this may seem counterintuitive, it is sensible and matches the teaching standard practice of 'retrieval practice' following undeniable research into the power of recall to place information into long-term memory from testing. Thus, it is hugely important how we feedback after and around tests.

Soapbox: *It galls me that students work hard for national tests such as GCSEs and get no feedback! We spend two to three years preparing students for an exam where the only feedback is a single level/grade. So, how do you, as a school or college, feed back from tests?*

You could write a book on this subject alone. It is a way of school life that needs to be deeply embedded in every department (and already probably is deeply embedded in every department – sometimes done well, sometimes not and is fear-inducing). Feedback needs to be a whole-school approach via the curriculum, underpinned by pastoral care with the wellbeing of a student at the heart of it. In highlighting the issue of how departments feedback for controlling test anxiety, it could take the form of a session at INSET or a series of staff meetings. This is the perfect blend for both academic and pastoral staff – it's about performance in tests and how we can nurture students to do their best. It needs to be part of a School Development Plan, actioned and monitored. (See Chapter 9 for a suggestion about School Development Plans).

As I have already suggested, a practical step is the sharing of data from the questionnaires at a staff meeting/INSET and a staff conversation about any anomalies. There should be an understanding that everyone can use this data in subtle and supportive ways. And, obviously, this data will not be shared in front of a class.

As a team, it's useful to discuss if there is a way to avoid negative peer comparison after a class test? How can feedback be managed so that meaningful targets for progress are absorbed? (This will depend on the whole school philosophy around taking tests and teaching to exams/fear appeals and the use of desirable difficulties.)

Is There Anything More Tutors or Teachers in Pastoral Roles Or Anyone Can Do?

Can you use internal systems/screens for positive test-taking ability messages? In my old school, we had 'study, test, test, test' on a loop on the internal TV. The students had received desirable difficulties training so that this was not an alarming message to a test-anxious student. They understood how their memories worked for taking exams.

Don't Call Study Periods 'Study' Periods; Call Them 'Recall' periods

Instigate a system in school where testing is cool. Failure is also cool. This is why changing the way your educational setting manages tests as a 'way of life' needs embedding.

> **Nitty Gritty**
>
> In giving students back control over taking tests, you will need to **revolutionize** the way you approach tests in your educational setting, as well as using the intervention/PSHE/Pastoral Scheme of Work. This is important and needs a whole school/college approach, which is why you have not only the intervention in this book (see Chapter 6) but also suggestions for a whole School Development Plan (Chapter 9).

Ideally …

So, let's assume you have and have had a steady drip of Growth Mindset assemblies. You have run a scheme of work on the most famous failures and famous people who fail, celebrated failure weeks and looked at the benefits that can come from failure. You have run the parents' evening and talked to them about how you are changing the school and avoiding fear appeals using cognitive science, desirable difficulties to give back control to the students. Your internal communication to students features the message 'study, test, test, test', and the use of cognitive science (retrieval practice/testing effect) is a performance management target for all teaching staff. You are on the way to a whole-school approach to giving students control about taking tests, but the intervention (now known as the PSHE/Pastoral Scheme of Work) is designed to intervene specifically. That is why the intervention needs delivering in a blanket way and as a strand of the PSHE/Pastoral curriculum. However, it cannot stand alone; the whole school needs to get behind this (see Chapter 9 for School Development Plan).

Further Thoughts and Suggestions

In all my years of teaching, I think the hardest aspect to manage in a classroom is peer comparison, especially if you've just given test results back. I have tried giving individual feedback from a test with some success while differentiated tasks continue in the classroom. I have tried to manage parental expectations with varying degrees of success. It can be very difficult for a student if their parent was academically successful and they aren't … yet! Then we are also fighting against the herd mentality that is very much a part of the teenage brain. I have always wanted to harness that herd mentality for good. I have suggested saying something positive to each other especially on WhatsApp so that students and their peers see positive affirmations written down. If this habit could be developed by a school among its youngsters and used prior to exams, it could be simply revolutionary. Instead of the 'OMG, I'm so scared, I haven't revised' common among peers before an exam – either verbally or in text – messages that say 'We trained well, we learned how memory works, and we just know this stuff' would feed into feelings of confidence about taking tests. To create mentalities like that from initiatives needs everyone involved and a whole school/college/parent approach.

So perhaps a key item on that school/college development plan needs to be positive affirmations about learning delivered to each other on a weekly basis. For exam year groups, they must be about exam revision strategies. There is definitely room for some more thinking around this idea and your setting could have tremendous creative thinking in finding ways to get students to emphasize the positive and reduce the negative – along with those other two conversations about how to manage all the exam processes and feedback!

Teens (and pre-teens) classify each other quickly (probably humans generally). Positivity towards each other exists within friendship groups (but can change on a daily basis). All it takes is an alpha (natural leader) in the group to say something positive and mainly, and the rest will believe and follow. The same can be said for a negative comment. You will be well aware of friendship dynamics and the power of Snapchat and WhatsApp. I just wish we could harness social media for more good than bad (bullying).

The intervention/PSHE/Pastoral is delivered to all students. It was most effective with students who have high test anxiety, but it helped all other students' wellbeing because it's a positive message and useful knowledge for life. All it needs is that one student in the group to remind students with a positive message about how they have studied before an exam, and self-efficacy in taking tests for all could be an outcome.

Could this fall to student leadership roles in schools? How about a 'leader of positivity about exams' whose job it is to send out positive messages on school systems and/or social media, or a 'leader of memory and learning'?

In all cases, the intervention/Scheme of Work/Pastoral provides students with personal strategies they can use if they are anxious about taking tests.

SCENARIOS

Just before we conclude this chapter I'd like you to consider some students and teachers, and their circumstances. Based on what you have just read, think about the best course of action the school can take.

1. *Ben is joining your school in Year 7. He has a known history of anxiety – especially around tests – and his absence record is worrying. His mum is open with you and worried that the pressures of secondary school will be too much.*
2. *You have an ECT* (Early Career Teacher) *joining the staff in September and you are responsible for their induction. What information do you include about test-anxiety management/feedback in their induction?*
3. *As a Pastoral Lead in school, you can see that this research and the resources can really help the wellbeing of both the anxious and non-anxious students in your school. Some of your team are tired of 'new initiatives' and feel very time-pressurized. What can you do?*

Scenario 1: Suggestions for Ben's mum

- Tell mum about the PSHE/Pastoral Scheme of Work that is delivered to get students into good revision habits.
- Explain that you teach, at this school, how memory works for tests and that the whole school is committed to managing test anxiety.
- Tell her that there is a whole School Development Plan that focuses on increasing students' self-confidence.
- Explain that there is a parents' evening coming up where parents will be trained in desirable difficulties so that they can support their children in effective study habits and help to manage any anxiety around tests by reminding their children of the 'study, test, test, test' motto.
- You can add that so many members of staff are trained on using desirable difficulties and *not* using fear appeals.
- The school is aware of the research on fear appeals and is committed to *not* using them with everyone.
- There is a working party investigating how, as a school, we can adhere to all the JCQ (Joint Council for Qualifications) rules while lessening the *impact* of the actual exam process in school.

Scenario 2: Suggestions for your ECT

- Explain there is specific INSET as part of the induction process on using desirable difficulties in teaching. You know that they have already covered retrieval practice, spacing and interleaving as part of the teaching standards, but this explains how the school setting tailors this to create an embedded culture that helps to fight test anxiety in school.
- Ask If they would like to be part of the working party that is leading this strand on improvements to students' wellbeing that is part of the whole School Development Plan.
- Ask what their experience is of students who are anxious about exams.
- Ask how they feed back after tests. Explain it's a real focus for the school, as this is where students appear to be suffering.
- Point them in the direction of this book and get them to suggest a response to this scenario!

Scenario 3: Suggestions for Pastoral Lead

- Using the content from this book, devise a 10-15 minute session (delivered at a regular time slot) that outlines the benefits of using the Scheme of Work for the students. Explain it is differentiated into year groups, and can be mixed and matched to suit less able and more able students by drawing on resources for lower or higher age groups.

- Explain that the resources are already created.
- It might be useful to have some student data with you so that you can share how many students are anxious in your setting.
- Give options on:

  1. how this can be run
  2. who can do it
  3. when it can be done.

- Explain it doesn't have to be them (*unless you want it to be* and then see above); you have two TAs/LSAs (for example) who are really interested in delivering this Scheme of Work.
- What you need to avoid is apathy, so it's important that whomever delivers the Scheme of Work has the 'buy in' to it – if it's not the whole team, then members of the team who are into this. As Pastoral Lead (I know how busy you are but also how committed to the students) you may well deliver the parent event but it doesn't have to be you.

I have given some ideas, but it will really depend on your setting and your team. I can't write for every situation that exists out there. The 'buy in' to improving the outcomes for the students is a deal breaker – whomever is delivering the Scheme of Work/talking to parents etc. needs to *want* to help. I ran this in a school. I went into a PHSE lesson for 20-30 minutes over a half term. That's all it needs. *That doesn't mean to say it should be you!* I asked the teachers if they wanted to stay or take a 20-minute break. Generally, they stayed, or a bit of both. There's no right or wrong way but you do need the enthusiasm for the topic.

Summary

In this chapter, you have learned what test anxiety is and where it comes from. The need for a whole school approach (I could argue a whole country approach to taking exams) needs to be adopted and current practice reviewed. The intervention is the PSHE/Pastoral curriculum included in Chapter 6, and the School Development Plans (Chapter 9) incorporates a whole-school approach to changing how tests are managed in your educational setting. You have discussed the research with parents and taught them about desirable difficulties, and you have your data about the students and their anxiety levels. The next steps involve staff training in the use of fear appeals followed by training in the use of desirable difficulties (Chapter 3) and possibly an investment in some attributional training for staff if you have not thought about this already in your setting.

Takeaways

- Test anxiety stems from trait and/or state anxiety about taking tests and the context students find themselves in.
- It is the educator's responsibility to try to ensure students feel confident about taking exams.
- Feeling confident in your ability (belief in capability) is more likely to improve performance in tests. This can be achieved in the same way that we would contextualize other areas of learning but in the case of exams it's through teaching students how memory works.
- By using desirable difficulties and through teaching the theory of it to the students we are allowing them to understand how their memory works for exams, and this can make them feel more confident about taking exams.
- Before we get to the desirable difficulties, it's salient to tackle the issue of fear appeals.

Homework

Here are some questions for you to answer. Make a note of your thoughts somewhere safe, or set up a discussion with others who may have read this chapter. Put yourself in the shoes of students as you work through. You will find other 'homework' throughout this book, which you can approach however works best for you.

1. What kinds of test anxiety are there?
2. What is self-efficacy?
3. Where does the PHSE/Pastoral Scheme of Work intervene?
4. How should the intervention be delivered?
5. What conversations does the whole school need to have?
6. How might a student with test anxiety feel?
7. What is a fear appeal?
8. What does your school do to manage test anxiety?
9. What could your school do?
10. Who needs the fear appeals and desirable difficulties training?

Memory Hotspot: *Moonwalking with Einstein*

I read a wonderful book by Josh Foer (2012): *Moonwalking With Einstein*. In it, the author talks about how memory athletes use pictures (sometimes rude ones) to remember the order of cards in multiple packs of cards. So, there is one tip but maybe not appropriate for all ages. The principle is elaboration, building cues of memory into the brain.

References and Further Reading

Alpert, R. & Haber, R.N. (1960). Anxiety in academic achievement situations. *The Journal of Abnormal and Social Psychology, 61*(2), 207-215.

Bandura, A. (1997). *Self-efficacy: The exercise of control.* Stanford University, CA: W. H. Freeman/Times Books/Henry Holt & Co.

Bjork, R. A. & Bjork, E. L. (2020). desirable difficulties in theory and practice. *Journal of Applied Research in Memory and Cognition, 9*(4), 475–479. UCLA Bjork Learning and Forgetting Lab. https://bjorklab.psych.ucla.edu/wp-content/uploads/sites/13/2021/01/RABjorkELBjorkJARMAC2020ForPostingSingleSpaced.pdf

Cizek, G. J. & Borg, S. S. (2010). *Addressing test anxiety in a high stakes' environment.* Thousand Oaks, CA: Corwin Press.

Csikszentmihalyi, M. (2008). *Flow: The psychology of optimal experience* New York: Harper Perennial Modern Classics.

Dweck, C. S. (2008). *Mindset: The new psychology of success.* New York: Ballantine Books.

Foer, J. (2011). *Moonwalking with Einstein: The art and science of remembering everything.* London: Penguin.

Liebert, R. & Morris, L. (1967). Cognitive and emotional components of test anxiety: A distinction and some initial data. *Psychological Reports, 20*, 975–978, https://doi.org/10.2466/pr0.1967.20.3.975

Putwain, D. W. (2020) Examination pressures on children and young people: Are they taken seriously enough? A provocation paper. The British Academy. https://medium.com/reframing-childhood-past-and-present/examination-pressures-on-children-and-young-people-are-they-taken-seriously-enough-e274b9595d4

Putwain, D. W. & Best, N. (2011). fear appeals in the primary classroom: Effects on test anxiety and test grade. *Learning and Individual Differences, 21*(5), 580–584. https://psycnet.apa.org/doi/10.1016/j.lindif.2011.07.007

Putwain, D. W., Remedios, R. & Symes, W. (2016a). The appraisal of fear appeals as threatening or challenging: Frequency of use, academic self-efficacy and subjective value. *Educational Psychology, 36*, https://doi.org/10.1080/01443410.2014.963028

Putwain, D. W., Symes, W. & Remedios, R. (2016b). The impact of fear appeals on subjective-task value and academic self-efficacy: The role of appraisal. *Learning and Individual Differences, 51*, 307–313. https://doi.org/10.1016/j.lindif.2016.08.042

Putwain, D. W. & Aveyard, B (2018a). Is perceived control a critical factor in understanding the negative relationship between cognitive test anxiety and examination performance? *School Psychology Quarterly, 33*(1), 65–74. Advance online publication, https://doi.org/10.1037/spq0000183

Putwain, D. W. & Symes, W. (2018b). Does increased effort compensate for performance debilitating test anxiety? *School Psychology Quarterly.* https://psycnet.apa.org/doi/10.1037/spq0000236

Spielberger, C. D., Anton, W.D. & Bedell, J. (1976). The nature and treatment of test anxiety. In M. Zuckerman & C. D. Spielberger (eds), *Emotions and Anxiety* (pp. 317–341). Mahwah, NJ: Lawrence Erlbaum Associates Inc.

Spielberger, C. D. & Vagg, P. R. (1995). Test anxiety. A transactional process model. In C. D. Spielberger & P. R. Vagg (eds.), *Test anxiety, theory, assessment and treatment.* (pp. 3–14) London and New York: Taylor & Francis.

Weems, C. F., Scott, B. G., Taylor, L. K., Cannon, M. F., Romano, D. M., Perry, A. M. & Triplett, V. (2010). Test anxiety prevention and intervention programs in schools: Program development and rationale. *School Mental Health: A Multidisciplinary Research and Practice Journal, 2*(2), 62–71. https://doi.org/10.1007/s12310-010-9032-7

Weems, C. F., Taylor, L. K., Costa, N. M., Marks, A. B., Romano, D. M., Verrett, S. L. & Darlene Brown, D. M. (2009). Effect of a school-based test anxiety intervention in ethnic minority youth exposed to Hurricane Katrina, *Journal of Applied Developmental Psychology, 30*(3), 218–226. https://doi.org/10.1016/j.appdev.2008.11.005

Wren, D. G. & Benson, J. (2004). Measuring test anxiety in students: Scale development and internal construct validation *Anxiety, Stress and Coping, 17*(3), 227–240. https://doi.org/10.1080/10615800412331292606

Zeidner, M. (1998) *Test anxiety: The state of the art.* New York: Springer Science+Business.

Zeidner, M. (2014). Anxiety in education. In R. Pekrun & L. Linnenbrink-Garcia (eds), *International handbook of emotions in education* (pp. 265–285). London, New York: Routledge, Taylor & Francis Group.

Zeidner, M. & Matthews, G. (2005). Evaluation anxiety. Current theory and research. In A. J. Elliot & C. S. Dweck (eds.), *Handbook of competence and motivation* (pp. 141–160) London, New York: The Guildford Press.

2 Fear appeals

> **What to Expect**
>
> *In this chapter we cover fear appeals, what they are and what they mean to test-anxious students, some students scenarios, extent of research into using interventions to manage test anxiety, ideas for audit of current practice and some personal experiences about how schools 'rev up' for exams.*

> **Key Terms**
>
> **blanket fear appeals:** treating every student as if they will fail the exam unless they put some hard work in
>
> **blocks:** how we teach in physical departments called blocks, blocks of subject, but think what blocking really means
>
> **creating a culture of testing:** audit what you do and what you can do, especially around feedback from exams

In the previous chapter, I refer to the initial steps an educational setting should take to engage parents in the process of giving students back control over test anxiety and I mentioned training staff, parents on the use of fear appeals and desirable difficulties so, before we move onto desirable difficulties, it is important to consider practice around high-stakes tests/exams in schools.

Personal Experience

For many years, I was an examiner for AQA (Assessment and Qualifications Alliance) at GCSE level. I loved the work – bit sad, I know, but it was truly the best professional development I had undertaken. I taught my GCSE classes afterwards with such fervour! I wasn't alone.

The KS2, KS3 (remember Y9 SATs!), KS4 and KS5 teams and in the independent sector (with its scholarship and school entrance papers) all 'revved' up to these key exam teaching points of the year. Mock exams, progress tests, more mocks. When your subject results are subject to scrutiny and pay may also be linked – it's important. There are always the standards meetings for you to explain your results to a member of the leadership team who in turn has to explain results to the governing body. All in all, it's pretty stressful for everyone then, isn't it?

The reason I came into this research area and spent five years studying and teaching at the same time is because I watched students crumble at all exam times of the year, including mocks.

As a teacher, I loved the lead-up to the exam season. As a head, I dreaded it. I had to manage the 'fall-out', students, teachers and parents' stress. Then there's the process, the exams officer managing often complex logistics, JCQ (Joint Council for Qualifications) rules and inspections. As a teacher, I would be getting into the exam run-ups with testing and marking; we have to do it because the content is so heavy and, to be fair (as teenagers say), there is just so much to absorb and learn. I would be firing on all cylinders. In the lead-up to exams, the tense atmosphere in schools becomes palpable. Mock exams and exams and teachers teaching in the lead-up to exams causes stress in a school setting.

I watched students (and staff and parents) crumble. I will keep saying this because that is what I witnessed repeatedly and with all age groups. The weeks around mocks and exams were torturous for many. Students would often come to me and say: 'Miss, I'm really stressed. Sir gave us this test and I couldn't do it. I don't like it when the results are handed back in class. I can't do it!' Staff would be tearing their hair out over results in the staff room and parents at the gate would say 'I'll be pleased when this is all over!'

You know, it's easier to stay at home than go through this!

This is the system we are in though at present and I'm not holding out for any change. As I mention in the conclusion of this book, I would love nothing better than for this book to become redundant because we have scrapped the current archaic methods of educating and assessing the ability of our youngsters. Students are required to take high-stakes tests and teachers are held to account for their results. Knowledge is fitted into boxes of possible usefulness and Ken Robinson's point about schools educating students out of creativity (Robinson, 2011) is a thought I always return to.

Soapbox moment – talking about boxes: *The antiquated 'boxiness' of the UK curriculum taught in rooms that are 'the Geography room' or the 'Maths corridor' is limiting. One place to start the change may be to change the physical spaces we restrict subjects to in order to expand our thinking. But there's no point if the curriculum has to be taught in* **blocks** *that is timetabled in blocks and the associated thinking is therefore in blocks and another meaning for the word 'block' is …… (you can fill the gap in!).*

It's not surprising then that many teachers, students and parents use fear appeals around exam times.

Fear appeals

Fear appeals are statements or comments made by teachers, peers and parents to students prior to high-stakes tests. They are designed to alert students to the importance of the upcoming test and the need to study hard, to prepare. Fear appeals use reminders of what is at stake – such as university or school entry, scholarships or academic record. Fear appeals may be meant to be helpful in motivating study prior to examinations but they may also affect self-belief. Putwain et al. (2014) suggest that for students who have high test anxiety, fear appeals made them more anxious. However, for students who have low test anxiety there are approximately 10–20% of the class who experience high test anxiety (Putwain and Daly, 2014). Remember, we don't want that to be a statistic, it needs to be our motivation for change.

Fear appeals **should not be** used in a blanket fashion to a class. Within that class there will be some students for whom hearing a fear appeal raises their anxiety levels about taking a test unnecessarily. The data that you have from the test anxiety questionnaires will show you the students who are the most anxious and the most confident about taking tests. Generally speaking, the students who may respond to a fear appeal are those that have come across in the data as the most confident but who you (as staff) know are not doing any work and have not been achieving their potential. An alternative to issuing **blanket fear appeals** is to target these students specifically to alert them in order to motivate them.

> ### In a Nutshell
>
> Targeted fear appeals can work for the over-confident and lazy but *terrify* the anxious students and should never be delivered in a blanket fashion. However, the intervention/PSHE/Pastoral Scheme of Work (Chapter 6) *should* be delivered to all in a blanket fashion as it is a positive process that can help the wellbeing of all students.

As said, I can recall time and time again groups of students male and female who came to see me desperate with what they were being told and asked to do around mock exam time; the use of fear appeals by teachers. It would often be a particularly heavy content subject where the students did expect to be tested but as the exams approached the teacher would be getting 'revved up' and the tense atmosphere in the classroom would therefore be getting 'revved up'. A huge part of the anxiety was often down to how these test results were then shared in class. For an anxious teen to have their results discussed in front of peers can be mortifying. In your setting are there subjects and teachers who manage this well? If so, seek these excellent practices out, especially if you think there is a problem around the feedback of tests. There may be a training need. There may be a line management issue. You may not be facing any problems with feedback after tests; I hope that is the case for you. However, experience has shown me, over many years, that many students are suffering with the problem of handling test feedback.

Soapbox: *The change in culture of an educational setting that I suggest (rethink the exam process!) would certainly help with the issue of test anxiety. If we changed the way we educate and assess our young, the problem might be gone forever.*

As educators, we know that the lockdowns have exacerbated teen anxiety. We know that school refusal is common and yet there will still be many classrooms in the land where teachers are using fear appeals because they have always done. (This is quite a pattern in schools – we've always done it this way!) There is an issue of training here. Given that this book includes a Scheme of Work (the intervention) for a whole new strand of PSHE/Pastoral care (Chapter 6), and is based on the latest research and used the best practice of retrieval practice, there will need to be a school/college focus on teacher training of these materials. It is important that you look at how you feedback after tests/mocks etc. As part of this there will be a need to deliver teacher training on the use (or non-use) of fear appeals and to gather (audit) current practice around teaching for exams in order to change practice in your setting.

Use the following chapters to help.

1. Chapter 9, for a suggested whole school development plan to embed the change in culture around taking tests.
2. Chapter 6, for the PSHE/Pastoral Scheme of Work, which is effectively the intervention.
3. Chapter 8, for a suggested teacher training programme for 'in-house' CPD for teachers or to parents.

Nitty Gritty

For times to change and for educational settings to give students control over taking tests, make them feel more self-efficacious; the use of blanket fear appeals in classrooms *must stop*. Given the current state of the mental health of many young people in our country, we all have a responsibility to stop pushing our kids to the edge!

Let's consider how fear appeals may impact students in your classroom.

SCENARIOS

These can be used for staff training purposes – without the solutions part! These are hypothetical scenarios and bear no relation to students I have met.

Scenario 1

Flossie is an anxious student. This is known to all staff. She has very high scores indicating test anxiety from the questionnaires. The anxiety is trait anxiety and has manifest-

in extreme forms. Flossie suffers from a severe lack of self-esteem, eating disorders and agoraphobia. The trait anxiety is exacerbated when she takes exams as she absorbs the context in the lead-up to exams and from the exam room itself. Flossie finds the exam room overwhelming and the atmosphere too stressful. There are already separate conditions set up for when Flossie is taking exams, and she sits them in a separate room with a teaching assistant. Everyone knows she is anxious, but teachers have still got to teach the content for the exam. There still needs to be mock exams and preparation for exam questions and getting to know the rubric. The results of mock test papers are a constant source of distress to Flossie even though she is doing well on them, she never feels it is good enough.

How can a school manage this situation?

While the arrangements for the actual taking of exams have been thought through and the SENCo has been busy with the exams officer in organizing this, it is the lead-up, in school, that is distressing Flossie the most.

The intervention delivered through PSHE/Pastoral lessons (see Chapter 6) will help Flossie. There are other actions a school can take: remind all staff regularly about who their most anxious students are and to *not* use fear appeals in a blanket fashion in classrooms; and remind staff to consider carefully how they will feed back from mock tests that are happening in the lead up to exams. Can they provide opportunities for individual feedback? How can they create a culture where students are not comparing their results to their peers? How can the school support them as teachers in this? Can a separate arrangement be made for feeding back to the most anxious students in the class? And how can this be managed so the anxious student does not feel a spotlight on them and does not stand out from their peers?

Scenario 2

Dilwar's test anxiety questionnaire scores surprise staff. He appears to be very anxious about taking tests, which is not something that has been apparent in class. He is popular and often jokes around with his friendship group. They are mainly high achievers but can be a bit lazy and, as a group, are regularly reminded by teachers about the importance of working hard. At parents' evening, Dilwar's mum and dad are hugely supportive and very keen for Dilwar to become a medic, like his brothers.

What actions should a school take here?

One possible route to take once the test-anxiety data was revealed is for the school to establish a mentoring programme for the students who showed the highest scores for test anxiety. This could be led by the SENCo/leadership/tutor team? Individual meetings might be held with the students to ask them why they feel so anxious. When Dilwar agreed to chat with his chosen adult, his form teacher, he revealed that he was working hard but felt enormous pressure to go into medicine; he wasn't sure that's what he wanted, but his parents – although supportive of him – had always expected this. The parents were called to a meeting (along with other students' parents for whom anxiety levels about taking tests were a surprise) and, with Dilwar there, the situation was discussed gently. In order for Dilwar to do his best and even secure a place at medical school, he needed to feel less anxious. While he was revising (as per the 'study, test, test, test' model that the school recommended) and was well supported, eating well and getting rest, he was under too much pressure to succeed. If he was going to succeed, the parents would need to start to reassure Dilwar that they would be happy no matter what; that exams aren't the 'be all and end all'. His parents really should have been saying this all along – encouraging gently but not placing their expectations first. Dilwar is a good student and works hard regardless.

Dilwar's teachers need to be briefed and not compare him to his brother, who was head boy in the school and went to Oxford to do medicine. The brother was confident and loved exams. They must not use comparison or fear appeals in front of Dilwar.

Scenario 3

Dawn came out as middle of the road from the questionnaires. She didn't seem to want to commit to the answers and answered mainly 2s on the Children's Test Anxiety Questionnaire. Her achievement in class has been mainly average. Other academic data held on file suggests she could achieve the top grades. Her tutor has raised her as a cause for concern in her year group as she has been regularly absent from school and is often late to lessons.

What actions should the school take here?

When the school has chased the absences with parents, there is always a reason, but Dawn's form tutor thinks it's more a case of mum liking to keep her daughter at home. The priority does not seem to be Dawn's education. This is a case where a 'fear appeal' might work. Dawn is not suffering with anxiety, and parents and Dawn need to understand that she must do some work if she wants to go on to college or she could face resits.

Scenario 4

Andrew doesn't do any revision for tests in school. His test anxiety questionnaire suggests that he is actually very anxious about tests. He's popular with his friends and can be a bit of a leader in his group.

What actions should the school take here?

Why doesn't Andrew do any revision? Does he know how to? It transpires that he's got a reputation with the peer group for not caring about his work. He has cultivated this reputation because he is actually terrified of exams or rather failure and so he adopts a sort of 'learned helplessness' (Seligman and Maier, 1967) approach. He doesn't revise because it's easier to explain failure this way than working and not succeeding because of his anxiety. His self-efficacy, his belief in ability to take tests, is severely compromised.

The intervention PSHE/Pastoral Scheme of Work will help (Chapter 6). He can learn how to learn so that he feels more confident about his abilities. However, the role he has adopted in the group is more difficult to break. It will mean that the whole group needs to be behind his new attitude. It's possible that this is where the whole School Development Plan comes in. Teachers are experts at talking to students and a group chat here about being mutually supportive of each other especially around the new scheme of work in PSHE/Pastoral might work. Alternatively, giving Andrew a student leadership role in promoting positivity around exams might help. Teaching students to learn how to learn and relating this to avenues outside of school life may contextualize the experience and make it more relatable for this group. Relate the learning and the exam process to learning to drive for example, and try to hook this group's attention this way.

Creating a Culture and Climate of Testing

Low stakes tests should be a part of every subject curriculum so that a high-stakes test becomes just another test ... although it's not, and students are not daft! But if testing is 'normalized' from an early point in school life, then a bigger test becomes simply that, a bigger test. Rather than students bemoaning, e.g. 'we've got a test in Physics, Chemistry, Maths this week', it should be regular practice, disguised as a quiz. Counterintuitively, for teachers, testing more will remove some of the emphasis on testing – unless it is accompanied with fear appeals. Recall of information is 150% more effective than other types of learning (see Chapter 3). Therefore if tests are normalized and fear appeals reserved for those who need them, then a high-stakes test should feel less stressful.

The exam room and use of invigilators can raise anxiety levels. To overcome this, some teaching and even better 'recall' (renamed from study period) sessions should take place in the 'exam room' so that students are used to recalling information in there. It's important to try to normalize this room too. Clearly, Flossie has separate arrangements so she should practise recall in that room, but it's possible that if she were taught and revised in the exam hall, she may feel more comfortable sitting an exam in there.

I am reminded of the excitement of the visualizer when I was teaching at a primary level – a way of sharing a student's work (primary school) in class. It was simply mortifying for many students. Some bright and able students loved the attention; many others dreaded it. How we spotlight children or find way for them to avoid the spotlight is key in making them feel comfortable in school and therefore able to function and do their best (and want to come to school!)

> **Nitty Gritty**
>
> Schools really are 'social experiments' and many students struggle in the collective atmosphere. It is up to us to find a way to support all students and the giving of feedback about tests is a crucial area to focus on.

Research About Using Intervention to Control Test Anxiety

There is very little research into test anxiety interventions in this country and even less on using retrieval practice (the testing effect or using low stakes tests in class) to control test anxiety. (More of this in the next chapter.) However, there is some research about using low stakes tests to ward off test anxiety from the USA using quite a large sample and across a wide age range.

A recent paper is a meta-analytic review of whether using quizzes/practice tests promotes or reduces test anxiety from Yang, Li, Zhao, Luo and Shanks (2023). The authors say that this area of research is in its infancy and conclude that testing reduces test anxiety.

Agarwal et al. (2014) surveyed 1,408 US middle and high school students (11- to 15-year-olds) and the results suggest that 72% of middle and high school students felt that retrieval practice helped them in exams. They suggest classroom teachers should adopt retrieval practice to manage test anxiety.

This research by Agarwal et al. (2014) has been featured on the Effortful Educator blog. Although retrieval practice is now included in the Initial Teacher Training Core Framework (2020) (https://www.gov.uk/government/publications/initial-teacher-training-itt-core-content-framework#:~:text=The%20initial%20teacher%20training%20(%20ITT,and%20delivering%20their%20ITT%20programmes) and on websites such as Learning Scientists. Org (https://www.learningscientists.org/) and Agarwal's retrievalpractice.org (https://www.retrievalpractice.org), there is very limited literature about the links between using retrieval practice and its role in reducing test anxiety.

A quick Google search in May 2024 for 'retrieval practice and test anxiety' resulted in the following:

- the Agarwal paper and using retrieval practice to reduce test anxiety (Agarwal et al., 2014)
- a blog from the Learning Scientists by Megan Sumeracki (https://www.learningscientists.org/blog/2020/6/25-1)
- the piece by the Effortful Educator, and
- a short piece by Teacher Toolkit.

My doctoral research is also listed (https://www.repository.cam.ac.uk/items/56ba1b4f-81ce-4f1f-acc5-10bc6d5a8aa1) and I can refer you to the paper I wrote with my supervisor (Barsham and Ellefson, 2020).

In short, there is little research in the UK other than the extensive research that is presented to you here in this book that was carried out in classrooms in the UK with real students, and delivered quickly and easily by a teacher.

I must make the point again here that my research is different from the above list as it is about retrieval practice of a wellbeing mantra 'your testing routes are well-oiled' and not subject content, but I draw heavily on the principles of retrieval practice/the testing effect to ensure that positive messages about the revision that has used desirable difficulties is remembered.

A Good Next Step: Step 2 – Audit of Current Practice

You will need to conduct an audit of current practice around exams in your school. How are fear appeals used? How can you change this? There must be a move away from blanket fear appeals in the classroom. You have already guided parents regarding this (see Step 1 in Chapter 1) and some work on peer groups in schools about using positive conversations not negative. In addition, you have placed positive visual reminders on screens, on forums and in assemblies – wherever and whenever to reinforce positive affirmations from the PSHE/Pastoral intervention. Importantly, a larger discussion needs to take place about how feedback is being delivered to students about tests. How are your anxious students responding when you hand them back papers? How can you manage this optimally?

You need a culture where testing for exams is considered normal. The only way to do this is to regularly use low- and high-stakes tests and to eradicate fear of failure, fear of peer comparison and a mindset that values feedback for what it is – an opportunity to improve. The School Development Plan (Chapter 9) is designed to support your thinking around this.

Another good place to start is with the Teaching Standards. It might be a while since some staff have viewed them and they have changed to include retrieval practice, which is the cognitive tool that we used to reduce test anxiety in schools.

> **Nitty Gritty**
>
> A reminder why we are doing this. Test anxiety will affect between 10% and 20% of all students in a school. Most high-stakes data (exam results) for the test anxious student will be skewed and not a real representation of their ability. Life choices are affected by performance in exams. We are intervening at the cognitive level or Box 2 of the model (see Figure 1.1 in Chapter 1) in order to try and give back control to students who are taking high-stakes tests.

Takeaways

- Think about fear appeals and when they may be used but come away from blanket fear appeal statements in classrooms because it makes anxious students more anxious.
- This is easily said and should be easily done but habits are hard to break and there may be a training need for some teachers who teach exam syllabuses.

- It will start with the whole school discussion about how test feedback is managed in school and an audit of current practice and its outcomes and proposals for the new practice and the benefits of this.
- So, after the parents' evening and the launch of the new School Development Plan that features a section on giving students back control over tests in order to improve their wellbeing around tests, and training teachers in desirable difficulties and fear appeals hopefully along with some attributional training (see Chapter 1), there needs to be an audit of how you are managing feedback from tests in your setting.
- It's not an overnight process. It's not a tickbox exercise because you are creating a culture of change. You need to normalize taking tests and the only way to do this is as a whole school. It's from the bottom up and from the beginning to the end, and it means training staff/parents on how memory works for testing and implementing this for the students.
- You are provided with the resources. Your school now needs the will and the passion for improving outcomes for students who are anxious about tests – with the added benefit that all students will experience increased wellbeing around test-taking.

Homework

Answer these questions.

1. What does the school need to audit?
2. How can the scenarios in this chapter be used?
3. Do fear appeals ever work?
4. Who is responsible for making testing better in school?
5. Is it a good idea to test more or less?
6. How can the teaching standards be used?
7. Do teachers like exams?

In Chapter 3, we come to the seminal work of Bob Bjork, Karpicke, Roediger, Dunlosky, Agarwal and many others about the power of using the 'testing effect' or retrieval practice for learning. I will then explain how we used this body of positive literature with the body of literature around test anxiety and self-efficacy to create an intervention that forms part of the School Development Plan, a PSHE/Pastoral curriculum and a 'to do' list that gets the ball rolling as practical steps for you to follow – although we have made a good start!

Memory Hotspot 1: Memory Palaces

If you have watched recent episodes of *Sherlock Holmes* on British TV, you will know about the memory palaces or places even that he uses. The programme often shows visual images of Holmes searching places in his mind, which is where he has observed information. It's like a visual photographic memory. This is the same idea presented in pages 193–194 of *Make it Stick* in which James Paterson, a psychology teacher, takes his class to the coffee shop and they mentally pin the content of the psychology to be learned around the room. In an exam then, one just has to remember the places and recall the associated content!

Memory Hotspot 2: Spelling Rocks!

I tried this idea of memory palaces when I was teaching spellings to a Year 5 class. It's difficult to teach because there are so many exceptions to the rules. I devised a system called 'spelling rocks' and painted various rocks (in gloss paint, so weatherproof) with spelling patterns on them, then placed the rocks around the school grounds. With each rock were worksheets on the spellings, instructions and examples. Spelling became fun as different groups each week set off to find different spelling patterns, which I managed like a treasure hunt. I explained, back in class, that they could then just picture the location and remember the spelling pattern they had found there. By moving the students from the classroom and making it fun, this created some elaboration of information to be cued into memory.

References and Further Reading

Agarwal, P. K., D'Antonio, L., Roediger, H. L., McDermott, K. B. & McDaniel, M. A. (2014). Classroom-based programs of retrieval practice reduce middle school and high school students' test anxiety. *Journal of Applied Research in Memory and Cognition, 3*(3), 131–139. https://doi.org/10.1016/j.jarmac.2014.07.002

Barsham, H. & Ellefson, M. R. (2020) Can teaching upper primary about the testing effect increase feelings of confidence about test taking? *Journal of the Chartered College of Teachers, Impact 8.* /

Brown, P. C., Roediger, H. L., McDaniel & M. A. (2014). *Make it stick: The science of successful learning.* Cambridge, MA: The Belknap Press of Harvard University Press. https://doi.org/10.1080/00220671.2015.1053373

Putwain, D. W., Daly, A. L. (2014) Test anxiety prevalence and gender differences in a sample of English secondary school students, *Educational Studies, 40*(5), 554–570. https://doi.org/10.1080/03055698.2014.953914

Putwain, D. W., Shah, J. & Lewis, R. (2014). Performance-evaluation threat does not adversely affect verbal working memory in high test-anxious persons. *Journal of Cognitive Education and Psychology, 13*(1), 120–136.
https://doi.org/10.1891/1945-8959.13.1.120

Putwain, D. W., Chamberlain, S., Daly, A. L. & Sadreddini, S. (2014). Reducing test anxiety among school-aged adolescents: a field experiment. *Educational Psychology in Practice, 30*(4), 420–444. https://doi.org/10.1080/02667363.2014.964392

Robinson, K. (2011). *Out of our minds: Learning to be creative.* Chichester: Capstone.

Seligman, M. E. P. & Maier, S. F. (1967). Failure to escape traumatic shock. *Journal of Experimental Psychology, (74*(1), 1–9.

Yang, C., Li, J., Zhao, W., Luo, L. & Shanks, D. R. (2023). Do practice tests (quizzes) reduce or provoke test anxiety? A meta-analytic review. *Educational Psychology Review, 35*(3), Article 87. https://doi.org/10.1007/s10648-023-09801-w

3 Using Desirable Difficulties to Give Back Control

What to Expect

In this chapter, I'll cover the desirable difficulties of: varying practice, interleaving, spacing, the testing effect or retrieval practice. I will complain about blocking (see Key Terms). I'll introduce the New Theory of Disuse (have fun with this) and Judgements of Learning, Learning Biases and Metacognition. This chapter also includes a year group monitoring of a metacognition suggestion tracking sheet (as an additional tool to the PSHE/Pastoral Scheme of Work in Chapter 6) and an optimal revision/testing schedule. Finally, there are some scenarios for you to play with..

Key Terms

blocking: cramming – only useful if test is immediate otherwise it's like putting on a rucksack of knowledge and then forgetting it

cross-pollinate: mixing ideas up better to solve problems

desirable difficulties: interleaving, spacing, the testing effect, moving from room to room

forgetting is good: if you can't remember something and have to look it up, or ask or just try to remember, it's harder yes but more likely something you'll remember in the future

judgement of learning: your belief about what you know

knowledge biases: when you think you know something but you don't!

metacognition of learning: knowing how you know what you know

new theory of disuse: memory is like an attic, the more you recall the easier it is to find items near the loft door; lack of use means your items are getting dusty in the back of the attic

retrieval practice: aka, the testing effect (below)

the testing effect: repeated testing stores information in the long-term memory and is 150% more effective study method than re reading or highlighting

Desirable difficulties or at least **the testing effect** (also known as **retrieval practice**, an aspect of desirable difficulties), is now used as part of initial teacher training and many of you will have heard of the term 'retrieval practice'. It was a performance management target for all teaching staff in my previous school because it's so key to optimal outcomes for staff and students.

Bjork and Bjork's (2011) 'desirable difficulties' are changes in the learning context that create challenges for the learner but enhance long-term retention of the knowledge. In the wonderful book *Make it Stick* (Brown, et al., 2014), the authors refer to this as 'when the learning is harder, it's stronger and lasts longer'. You see, it is harder to try to change the way you learn and test yourself or have others test you than just reading and highlighting with a pen. The desirable difficulties' include the following.

Desirable difficulty 1: Varying practice conditions

The first difficulty is varying the conditions of practice – for example, the room used for studying (e.g. Bjork, 2011; Imundo et al., 2020; Smith, Glenberg and Bjork, 1978).

I have already suggested getting students to recall key information in the rooms where they will sit their high-stakes tests and *not* just for their mock exams. Regularly practising recall in the exam room may help with test anxiety because the student knows they have recalled exam content knowledge in that room before and therefore will be able to do this again. This will help with self-efficacy in taking tests.

How could you vary the conditions of practice in your subject area?

Spelling rocks

I taught spelling using 'spelling rocks', hiding spelling patterns under various rocks outside of the classroom. Students had to follow a treasure map with clues to find the rocks and then learn the spelling pattern they found under the rock, plus complete some spellings. It was fun and got the students moving. This method also used a bit of the principle of 'memory palaces'. Importantly, it varied the place of recall of the spelling pattern practice.

Desirable difficulty 2: Spacing study

The second DD is pacing study or practice (tests), interleaving – not **blocking** – and generating information retrieval.

Blocking is the same as cramming and is really the modus operandi of many students. And, it can work ... if the test is the next day. However, it is not information that has gone into the long-term memory. So, here is the reason why exams and our current testing regimes are so limiting. We have students trained to jump through hoops to get to the next level – a bit like rewards on a video game – it's addictive stuff, the next level, but then they are not really learning for life. They are learning for tests, and the problem with this is that while they may do OK in the next-day test, they wouldn't if the test was later, in a few weeks' time, and if they need to access that information later on in their lives to solve a world problem – the knowledge has gone.

> **Nitty Gritty**
>
> We are really limiting our students' abilities to problem solve by testing them in the way that we currently do. Our students are very conditioned to 'blocking' or 'cramming'. They feel good about it. They feel as if they have revised well if they've read a passage 20 times and get top marks on a test. Of course! However, if they were to take that test again in six weeks' time, most of the knowledge for most people would not be retained. This is the problem with cramming or blocking. It's a short-term high.

If we consider the medical profession for a moment with the stresses and strains placed on them to remember, recognize and assimilate information to diagnose and treat, this can only be done if the information is in the long-term memory and had not been crammed in for a test. Yes, we can access research and remedies easily, but technology can fail and a knowledge of fundamentals is always going to be useful – potentially life-saving?

More on Blocking

Most of the research in this area explains that students are unable to give really good **judgements of (their) learning.** As said, many believe that re-reading and highlighting are effective revision strategies even when they are told and presented with information to the contrary (Dunlosky et al., 2013; Bjork and Bjork, 2019b).

Soapbox: *In most schools, we teach in subject 'blocks', the timetable in most schools is set into 'blocks', and the corridors and classrooms in our schools referred to as 'blocks'. I think we should just pause a moment to consider the meaning of the word 'block' to realize that this is what we are doing with the brilliant brains of our youngsters in the current UK educational system of GCSEs and A levels.*

It's worth considering that the synonyms of 'block' are 'to hinder', 'impede', 'obstruct'! By insisting on the antiquated curriculum of GCSEs and A levels, we are binding our youth to **blocks of education** and teaching them how to focus on one subject that there is then a high-stakes test in. This may have been appropriate in the past when jobs were for life, but advances in technology and an internet means that many students will 'do' multiple jobs and do them at the same time.

> **Nitty Gritty**
>
> We need to encourage thinking that can span different directions and pick out the relevant parts from different subjects, make links and synthesize information to solve problems. We can't teach this while we are wedded to the 'blocks' of education. Cross-pollination of ideas is crucial for solving problems and the world has some pretty big problems to solve; what's more, we are educating generation after generation out of the idea of cross-pollinating ideas by teaching them in blocks about blocks and testing in blocks. Blockheads!

The only time this idea of a cross-curricula approach seems to manifest in schools is in the Early Years Framework and also in 'topic' work in primary schools and the International Baccalaureate. It is not standard practice to **cross-pollinate** for older students in most schools. As soon as we can, we start to deliver subject specialisms in blocks and insist on mastery of content before another subject can be covered. We do educate our youngsters out of thinking outside the box in the very fabric of how schools, timetables, courses, exams and textbooks are designed and curricula administered, teaching taught and students examined.

Let's return to DD2 and its components of 'interleaving and spacing', which means: mixing up the learning, letting some forgetting of a subject set in before going back to it; and (for a student) perhaps not achieving mastery but moving onto another topic. Maths teachers look away, but it might be helpful for a student to move onto another topic before they have mastered another. Move onto 'shapes' before 'decimalization mastered'! When revising, students should mix up their subjects. **Forgetting is good!** Blocking is bad! Forgetting is good because it makes the memory work harder to remember and then this effort will result in knowledge that goes into the long-term memory (Bjork, 2011).

Bob Bjork describes how memory works in this great short video in a great short video on YouTube (search for Episode 5 ✚ Learning to Learn: Uncut Conversation with Bob Bjork).

Essentially, we are not computers that can regurgitate input information – well, at least we can for one day but not subsequent days. Memory likes things such as cues and links and elaboration. Memory athletes remember huge swathes of information by associating decks of cards with (often rude) imagery. We need patterns, pegs (hooks to hang ideas/imagery on) and mnemonics to remember because we are not computers.

By interleaving subjects, we are effectively creating cross-curricular thinking and we're making the learning harder. Teachers will resist because we insist on testing the students in a 'blocked' exam and there is really so much content they have to cover; thinking History, Religious Studies GCSEs here, but there are more …

> **Nitty Gritty**
>
> Interleaving of learning means that students have to try to remember information and look up information they have forgotten, and that is when real learning happens. Learning that won't be forgotten and can be used in the future.

Blocking is like putting on a rucksack of knowledge and, once splurged on a test paper, it is removed. So, practical applications of desirable difficulties so far:

- Mix up revision timetables, which allows 'spacing' to happen naturally, and the twin of spacing and forgetting – forgetting is good; *that would be an excellent motto for a school*!

- Actually, even testing yourself on something you've never learned before and then looking up the answers cues the information far more effectively into the brain when inputted (Giebl et al., 2021).

The process of how interleaving and spacing can work to drive information into long-term memory is beautifully explained in a sports example in the book *Make it Stick* (Brown et al., 2014) with an example from Cal Poly (pp. 79–82). This is an example using baseball, so good for PE departments especially to consider but the principles apply to all subjects.

In a Nutshell

Two teams were trained in pitching a ball at a distance. Team A practised the same shots at the same length over and over again. Team B varied their practice. They interleaved some shorter and longer shots.

So: *Who was the best team at pitching the shot to the required distance after one week and after six weeks?*

You got it? After one week, team A were the best. They had only practised the one shot, so they nailed it. But when tested again after six weeks, team B were the best at the shot at the required distance but not just that one. Because they had varied their practice they nailed shots at all distances – it was in their long-term memory because although their practice was harder, it was stronger and lasted longer.

This is how revision works! Interleaving and spacing take time but knowledge is learned for a long time. Unfortunately, most teachers simply don't have time to teach their students how to learn like this – because of the tests ...

The effectiveness of desirable difficulties (Bjork and Bjork, 2011) have been examined by many experiments over the years and the results are overwhelmingly positive for using these ways of learning (e.g. Bjork and Bjork 2011; Karpicke and Roediger, 2008). Furthermore, Dunlosky et al. (2013) conducted a comprehensive survey on the effectiveness of ten different learning techniques. They observed students and their revision methods. Techniques such as re-reading, highlighting, keyword mnemonics, summarization and imagery use for text learning were found to have low usefulness whereas retrieval practice or testing and distributed (spaced) practice were found to have high usefulness.

Desirable Difficulty 3: The Testing Effect

Importantly, the 'testing effect' is designed to improve encoding of information going into the memory, thus improving the retention of that information (e.g. Bjork, 2011). The more elaborate the encoding of information as it goes into the memory, the longer the knowledge will last (Bjork, 1975). In a Nutshell shows some research data.

In a Nutshell

'study, test, test, test' is 150% more effective at retaining information to be learned than 'study, test, study, test, study, test' or

'study, study, study, test' (Roediger and Karpicke, 2006a).

In the PSHE/Pastoral Scheme of Work, there are opportunities for the students to carry out their own research using these principles.

Nitty Gritty

This is the key thing for our students to know: Information that is retrieved from memory (from testing oneself) can be recalled more easily in the future, including in an exam, than it would have been if you haven't tested yourself. (Bjork, 1975). It's simple: the more you test yourself, the easier it will be to remember the content you need. You won't have forgotten this. Now, this is important information for test anxious students whose brains may go into fight, flight and freeze mode through anxiety, to know! They need to remind themselves how they studied for the exam, how memory works and reassure themselves that the content/information that is needed is there.

This is the main idea behind the test anxiety intervention or PSHE/Pastoral Scheme of Work detailed in Chapter 6. Key to all of this is, rather than using fear appeals in class you are telling the students that 'your testing routes are well-oiled'. This phrase or saying explains, in simple terms, the retrieval process and was used by teachers in the research behind this book to successfully instill a sense of self-belief and self-efficacy in taking tests.

The Scheme of Work takes you through it, week by week and step by step. For the 'wanting-to-know-a-bit-more-of-the-research' folk out there, I'm sharing this wonderful theory by Bob Bjork called the **new theory of disuse** as a possible additional resource for you. I try to explain this theory using a metaphor. This could be used with your students too; alternatively, get them to draw what you are about to learn.

New Theory of Disuse (Bjork and Bjork, 1992)

Imagine that your memory is an attic. Every time you use a piece of knowledge it's like the door to the loft opening. It is easy to access or get out of the attic because it is placed near the door. Now, at the back of the attic is some knowledge from a year ago. You haven't needed this for some time, so it's just been left, gathering dust in the back. You're trying to remember it, but it's taking time – there is a lot of knowledge in the attic. Once you have accessed it, though, perhaps from looking it up and reminding yourself, you'll find it's easier to remember when you need it. It's because you brought it to the front of the attic and let it out of the loft door.

Using Desirable Difficulties to Give Back Control 39

Now, when you're revising for exams, you should regularly bring the knowledge to the loft door for all of your subjects. This way, all the piles of knowledge you need will be there and ready for you to get out of the loft – you just have to open the door. The way to do this is through interleaving and spacing and recalling the knowledge.

However, the optimal way to keep the information to hand or nearish the loft door is to have forgotten something, not totally so that it is at the very back of the attic but a bit of forgetting so that the knowledge is not quite at the loft door. Trying to bring this knowledge through remembering to the loft door is what memory really loves. Yes, it feels harder to try to remember something, but this is exercising the memory and making it stronger so that even knowledge placed in the middle parts of the attic can be retrieved. If you keep recalling the different piles of knowledge, you can work a system in your brain where you are maintaining access to all the information you need quite close to the loft door so that you can use it. Sometimes a mnemonic can help to trigger the pile of knowledge too. Let me try to explain this visually.

There was a comic strip in the *The Beano* a long while ago featuring the 'Numskulls' – deemed to be people who lived in the brain and organized such things as the 'eye' department, the 'ear' department and the 'brain' department. I can imagine them busy at work in the memory department, which is the area of the brain that we are concerned with. It may look something like Figure 2.1.

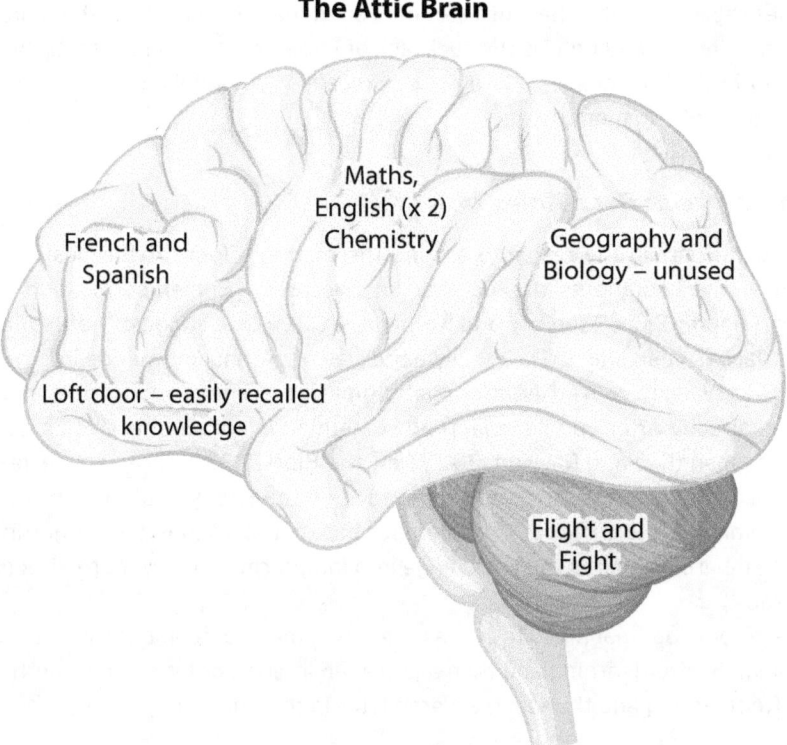

Figure 3.1 New Theory Of Disuse (Attic recall) – Flossie's Brain.
Source: FreePik

This is Flossie's brain. She is anxious about taking exams. She is studying Maths, English Language, English Literature, French, Spanish, Geography, Biology and Chemistry. Over the last 12 weeks, she has been following a revision schedule that she was taught about in PSHE/Pastoral lessons at school, which promotes mixing up the subjects. Most nights she studies three subjects for 30 minutes each by testing herself. There are two subjects she hasn't bothered with – Biology and Geography – as she has been re-reading chapters in class and summarizing them with her teacher. They also had a test a few weeks back. In addition, Flossie did quite well in her mock exams on these subjects. Flossie does put the time into languages, but they are tested every week in school on their vocabulary and grammar too.

As you can see, the weekly tests in languages plus the interleaved and therefore spaced revision has given Flossie really easy access to these subjects. When the GSCE results came out, Flossie had achieved well in all of her subjects apart from Geography and Biology, where she relied on chapter summaries and re-reading the content to revise. The languages were readily recallable, in spite of her anxiety, and the Maths, English and Chemistry a bit more difficult to remember. However, she had used a mnemonic for key information in these subjects and could readily recall it, so the learning had a peg (that mental coat hook you have linked something to so that you can remember it) to link her subject content from. She had tested herself a couple of times in Geography and Biology straight after re-reading a chapter, highlighting key points, and had done well in the test, so assumed she knew the content. This is where **metacognition of learning**, judgements of learning, is as key to teach as desirable difficulties because students are generally 'not good' at monitoring their own learning. The re-reading was the rucksack of knowledge put on for tests, but it wasn't at the front of the attic because it hadn't been recalled repeatedly over a period of time. It wasn't in the long-term memory.

The Testing Effect: Best Times to Test

There are guidelines in the research around the testing effect for the best time to test. Intricacies in the arguments are detailed in *Successful Remembering and Successful Forgetting,* Chapter 2, by Roediger and Karpicke (2011). Some suggest that testing directly after material has been learned is a really good way of getting knowledge into the memory and then twice weekly or weekly after that. Some researchers oppose this view and say that testing directly after you have learned something is not as effective as letting some forgetting happen (Pyc and Rawson, 2010; Pan and Bjork, 2021). For example, learning the content on a Tuesday but testing your knowledge on the Friday might mean you have forgotten more and that it is harder to remember but that ultimately this forgetting and the harder remembering secures the knowledge into long-term memory more effectively once remembered.

There are some optimal times to test as there is some debate about whether you should test immediately after learning and then again at an interval or let some forgetting happen straight after learning and then test, covered later in this chapter.

Anything teachers can do to make content more memorable will be appreciated by the memory, but the input of information must exist alongside using the testing effect or retrieval practice.

Testing on Unknown Content

Research has shown that even recalling incorrect information is better than no recall at all (Kornell et al., 2015) and recalling or doing a test (Bjork and Bjork, 2020) before you have the knowledge is effective at cueing the knowledge into the brain. I suggested this to some students in class: that we had a test on a topic they knew nothing about. They were filled with horror. But we did it anyway because there was no pressure or stress involved and no scores being recorded. It's really helpful to cue information into the brain this way because, as I was teaching the material afterwards, the students were like 'Oh yeah, OK, I see now' - and there is your memory peg. Testing on a subject not yet taught provides valuable cues into memory. What a great way to introduce a topic.

Metacognition of Learning and Knowledge Biases

How much time do we spend in schools/educational settings teaching students how to monitor their learning effectively? How do they know that they know what they know? Does a test score rally give the student and teacher accurate assessment data especially if revision has been blocked or crammed? How does your setting support metacognition of learning? There is a whole raft of research on judgements of learning and it is an interesting read that suggests most students are pretty bad at judging what they know (Bjork, Dunlosky and Kornell, 2013). The earlier example of Flossie is typical: 'I got full marks on a test in that last week, so I know it.' And fair enough. Unless students are taught the theory behind the testing effect and learn about how memory works, they will assume they know the material if they get full marks on a test having just revised the material and then not bother to revise this material again. They will not be aware that they are subject to *foresight bias* here.

It is important to teach students how they can learn to learn and how they can truly know what they know.

It is likely that times are changing since retrieval practice was added to the teaching standards in 2020, and it is possible that more students are aware of the power of testing. Bates and Shea (2024) suggest that retrieval practice is happening in UK classrooms. In the past, Kornell and Bjork (2009) state that relatively few students viewed testing as a learning event with most students viewing testing as a type of monitoring of what is known. It is at this core, initial point that students need to understand why they are being tested and testing cultures in school changed. Roediger, Agarwal et al. (2010, 2011) and Agarwal et al. (2010) suggest that, although it may seem counterintuitive to educators, education in school benefits from additional testing. This situation is because tests or quizzes, essays, exercises and effortful retrieval of information are powerful mnemonic devices. If students can understand this, then we are providing the context, the rationale for testing. If this is the school's mantra from when a student joins, then seeing tests as a negative, abhorrent experience to be suffered through might wane.

Nitty Gritty

Learning the knowledge about how memory works and how testing works on memory would help with metacognition and the ideas and principles behind students' often-incorrect *judgements of learning*. Often, students believe blocked practice (or repeated study) is better for learning than testing (e.g. Bjork et al., 2013), and students often use suboptimal learning strategies such a re-reading and highlighting (e.g., Dirkx et al., 2019; Dunlosky et al., 2013).

Examples that exist in the literature around judgements of learning include Roediger and Karpicke (2006b), who discuss this issue in an experiment about the meta-memory of prose passages. They found students' judgements of learning felt that repeated study was better than repeated testing. Bjork and Bjork (2019) discuss the benefits of interleaving (mixing it up and spacing it out) over blocking or massed practice for perceptual motor skills (such as learning different baseball strokes), verbal-conceptual procedural skills (learning algebra), and the long-term retention of knowledge and transfer skills. The benefits of interleaving were evident in all types of learning. However, even when the research was shared with the students in this experiment, they did not believe in the power of testing. Moreover, even when they knew the facts from the research that testing and interleaving was better than blocking or cramming, two-thirds of the sample said they would still use a blocked method of learning. You can take a horse to water …

Back to Blocking Briefly

One problem is the way schools and curricula are designed. From an early age – or at least once the awe and wonder of EYFS (Early Years Foundation Stage) has passed, we teach children in subject blocks. We teach 'in blocks', test 'in blocks', timetable 'in blocks', and situate classrooms 'in blocks', so is it any wonder students think that massed practice or blocking is best? We have drilled it into them, and we are limiting them. We are putting up barriers to their learning – we are quite literally blocking them!

Nitty Gritty

One of the main barriers to real metacognition for learning is about being allowed and having time to make mistakes. So many teachers are under pressure to run through content-heavy GCSE curricula to the extent that the issue of mistakes in learning cannot be given time. In this sense, the curriculum is actually adding to this idea of 'snowflake' children who can't face real life. There is simply not enough time in schools to allow students to think for themselves, work it out and solve the problem. Not enough time to reflect on what they know and what they need to know other than which chapters they haven't covered yet in a textbook.

Please Let Them Make Mistakes

There is a real need for mistakes in academic work to be celebrated and time given for effortful learning rather than simply getting through the content of a syllabus. However, for this to happen effectively, the way students are assessed needs to be changed to allow for less content and more, real learning. Misconceptions in Science learning are common (e.g., Tsapali, 2019), and slowing down and making more mistakes that can then be corrected along the learning journey may reduce some of these misconceptions. As previously stated, incorrect recall (with corrective feedback) is better than no recall at all (Kornell et al., 2009; 2015).

Metacognition

Teaching students about key aspects of how learning works is integral to developing learning and improving outcomes for students. I suggest teaching students about memory and how the testing effect (attic brain) works on memory, other memory techniques (see the memory hotspot later) and biases such as *foresight bias* and *hindsight bias*. If we were able to dedicate time to some of the educational theories, it is possible that this would reduce test anxiety and promote learning techniques for life. It is imperative that we treat the root cause rather than the symptoms. Students are anxious for many reasons. One is the volume of content-heavy subject material that they have to learn and regurgitate to pass a high-stakes exam that is a passport to another stage of life, but let us pause to ask: *What are we really doing here?* We're not even teaching students how to take tests or at least how the memory works when taking tests.

What better education could we give than actually teaching students how to learn?

A Note on Knowledge Biases

Foresight bias (Koriat and Bjork, 2006) is when easy recall of information, straight after reading a text, does not mean the information is learned even though the learner thinks they will be able to reproduce this information again easily. In other words, a student has learned something in class, been tested on it and performed well. They got a good mark! They think they know this and do not need to revise or re learn or recall this content again.

Hindsight bias (Fischhoff, 1975) is when we think we knew the information all along and this misconception can then affect what we study or learn for an exam. In other words, *I know that! I did a practice paper on that and got 90% so I don't need to learn it.*

Below is a suggested Metacognition of Learning overview (see Table 2.1) where an outline of what could be taught so students know how to monitor their learning. This is then supported by further ideas for getting students to truly understand their own learning. As stated at the beginning of the chapter, we should teach children about desirable difficulties (this is in the PSHE/Pastoral Scheme of Work, Chapter 6) but the other 'prong' in the 'attack' is to get students to monitor their own learning effectively. Therefore, this also needs some teaching (and thus teacher training). These are ideas only and as a school/

college you will be able to take this premise and tailor it to your setting and come up with far better ideas!

I have used GCSEs and A level exams in this example because they are the most common high-stakes tests, but please read and include here any BTech or Cambridge National or Functional Skills, or IB-level qualifications.

For students with individual needs, it has been shown that retrieval practice or the testing effect works well with students with low working memory (Agarwal et al., 2017). You will know your students and will be able to tailor any of the resources in this book to their needs.

The ideas about metacognition of learning could easily extend to higher education. As said, these are just suggestions and you can adjust to suit your setting and improve my suggestions. To do something like this will require three simple changes that are 'doable' in the school/college settings (see Chapter 9). It could make a big difference to how students perceive their learning and give them back control at a root level, which would hopefully grow up the tree and into the branches of feeling in control in the exam room on exam day.

1. Teach students (having trained teachers) about desirable difficulties and especially the benefits of the 'testing effect' or retrieval practice using the PSHE/Pastoral Scheme of Work in this book.
2. Rename study periods in school 'recall' periods and ensure they are used for testing/recall, not for re-reading.
3. Find a way of getting students to track their testing – not setting targets from one test to another, but tracking how often and how effective their own personal testing is (see the Monitoring of Learning column in Table 3.1). Then discuss this in pastoral time or however your individual setting thinks is best.

Table 3.1 Ideas for Promoting Metacognition of Learning in Your Setting

Year Group	Theory through PSHE/Pastoral Scheme of Work – see Chapter 6	Monitoring of Learning	Teacher Training Requirement
5/6	The testing effect – the power of testing, 'study test, test, test' is best	Self-reflection – reflective learning journal about different tests in different subject areas	Knowledge of the effectiveness of the testing effect (see teacher training materials, Chapter 8)
7/8	The testing effect, interleaving, spacing, changing rooms, elaboration (all the desirable difficulties)	Monitor and record when they use the different techniques; group discussions on effectiveness in PSHE/Pastoral time	Teacher training materials, Chapter 8; all the desirable difficulties, Chapter 3
10/11	The testing effect, desirable difficulties, monitoring of retrieval fluency, biases in learning	Use recall periods (study periods) to evaluate how they've been doing in tests, if they feel they have any **knowledge biases**	Pastoral support/time for discussion Keep a testing diary?
12/13	Desirable difficulties, the new Theory of Disuse, retrieval-induced forgetting	See Y10/11 use in recall periods for A level/IB subjects	Pastoral support in discussing testing – keep a testing diary?

An Example of Retrieval Practice and Spelling Tests

In this section, I write about an experiment that I was able to run in two primary school settings. Neither of the schools took SATs in Year 6. It may or may not be possible in your own setting, but I include this here because it's a good example to demonstrate the point about learning for tests vs learning for knowledge that will be used in life and importantly has actually been carried out in two real primary school settings.

Before I became a headteacher, I spent many years teaching secondary and primary English. Teaching spelling in primary schools usually consists of teaching the spelling pattern (and the exceptions to the rule), then sending students home with a list of words exemplifying that pattern to learn for the following week's spelling test. This test is then marked, scores noticed and 'stars' (or whatever) awarded. I noticed over a long period of time that the spelling test was really quite useless in helping students to spell correctly when they completed writing. You see, the spelling test is 'blocked' practice. Learn a pattern, test on it, then forget it. Students are learning for the test, not for writing. Therefore they do not apply the knowledge to their writing.

At this point, I'd like to thank the parents and staff who came on the journey with me as we turned the spelling test upside down!

As I suggested at the beginning of this book, one of the first steps is to talk to parents, to manage expectations. However, an important step just before talking to parents is to talk to staff who will be involved in the process. I held a staff meeting to talk about the issues with spelling and the principles of retrieval practice. Staff agreed that the weekly spellings test results were not reflected in subsequent written work and they agreed to trial the scheme. This was important, and I met with staff halfway through and at the end of the scheme to gather their feedback, along with feedback from students and parents. Once the support was enlisted, it was time to invite in the parents.

They were invited to a talk about desirable difficulties (Bjork and Bjork, 2011) and told that the '20 out of 20' correct spelling results may no longer apply. I explained that the learning would be 'harder but stronger and last longer' (Brown et al., 2014, p. 9). This is quite a hurdle for some parents to leap over. For a long time, not only children but also parents have been conditioned to block learning and the seemingly effective results the weekly spelling test brings. However, in my experience, parents readily see that the spellings are being learned for a test and the learning not applied subsequently. In my experiment, a parent survey of 29 out of 30 parents said they did not want to return to the old way of testing spellings.

Here is how it can work: Spelling lists for Years 1 to 6 are handed out, weekly as usual, but the testing interleaves the spellings from each week so that tests combined different weeks' spellings. Corrective feedback is always given. It is excellent practice to get students to look up any spelling mistakes (which can be pair or group work as well as individual), as this is encoding and elaborating the information into the brain more effectively than just writing out three times. What we found was that even repeated mistakes began to be spelt correctly after a few weeks. I recall a particular challenge for one of my students: 'astronaught'. It was spelt incorrectly for six weeks or thereabouts but once learned will never be spelt incorrectly again. I am confident in saying that.

Learning to spell this way takes longer to teach and learn but lasts for life. What is more important: getting 20 out of 20 on a test, which becomes meaningless because the content is forgotten as soon as the test is over, or learning how to spell 'astronaut' correctly?

Soapbox: *Learning for a test that receives no feedback, just a grade, and where the knowledge is largely forgotten afterwards is the premise that our current GCSE system runs on. Is that a reason to stick with meaningless spelling tests?*

This interleaved spelling testing system takes some monitoring, by the teacher, of the words tested in each week, and it made learning spellings harder. The retrieval is harder but the elaboration greater because of the opportunities to make mistakes and receive feedback, and therefore the learning lasts a lifetime!

I wrote about these ideas in a blog for learningscientists.org and although a little bit dated, you'll find the blog by searching 'Taughtology: The incorrect science of teaching wrongly'.

As mentioned in the blog, my trial at using desirable difficulties to teach spelling may not be that revolutionary and the successful *Speller* scheme (Horn and Ashbaugh, 1920; note the date) was 'onto' something after all. I think the main point is that as an educator who wants students to learn and retain knowledge, I was committed to the process of effortful learning and the promotion of making mistakes. Under the new interleaved spelling scheme, the learning that was happening was promoting a culture that it is alright to make mistakes and that learning to spell can take time but the learning lasts for a lifetime rather than a test. I do acknowledge that there isn't always time for making mistakes when having to deliver a content-driven syllabus and I think that this issue is a barrier to real learning. I have said that already and may do again!

Staff, students and parental feedback was overwhelmingly positive about the new spelling scheme. Student comments referred to the interleaving and how they used to just re-read their spellings, which made them feel secure before a test but that because they know that mixing spellings up is actually making their brains stronger and, one could argue, their resilience tougher, they thought the new spelling system was a good one for them.

> *This small spelling scheme experiment embodies large educational principles that could/should underpin a whole education system, but doesn't – yet!*

Nitty Gritty

Importantly, for students with test anxiety, cramming is one of the worst things they could do because they will be in a state of anxiety when they are trying to cram, so the information will not go into their memories due to their being primed with anxiety.

Up to this point, I have bemoaned the practice of cramming or blocking and noted the problem with **knowledge biases** as a result of doing well in a test that has been crammed for.

However, cramming or blocked practice works if the need to remember is for a short time such as a next-day exam. It's better than nothing but the cramming process can be anxiety inducing. The image of putting on a rucksack (backpack) of knowledge, using it in an exam and then taking it off has been mentioned previously – it can work but it is less than desirable!

Nitty Gritty

For a test-anxious student, knowing that previous recall aids recall in an exam situation, and that by testing themselves they have the knowledge they need stored in their long-term memory and can access this, that the knowledge is ready to go in an exam because 'the testing routes are well-oiled', brings about a feeling of control and gives self-efficacy in test-taking. This reduces worry and increases belief in capability. All students should know how memory works and how to study for life though, not just the anxious ones.

Hopefully, you can see it is imperative that a student who feels anxious about taking exams understands how memory works in order to avoid that anxiety?

As the PSHE/Pastoral Scheme of Work reveals, there are strategies that students who feel anxious about exams can use. One of these is self-talk and/or self-writing onthe knowledge about how memory works – a sort of reaffirmation about their revision process and this helps to bolster feelings of self-efficacy in test taking. That is half the battle. If a student feels they have control in an anxious situation, then they feel more capable. This is also why cramming is *not* a good idea for an anxious student because if a student is cramming information, then they are not in control. Each student is an individual and cramming may work for some, but it is an unlikely process to work for an anxious student.

Effort

Effortful retrieval is crucial for the testing effect to work (e.g. Butler and Roediger, 2007). In other words, cramming and then testing and doing well is a form of kidding yourself. One of the best ways to make sure the recall is effortful is to let some forgetting set in before you try to recall the information. This is because the brain likes elaboration and for information to be cued in. If a student can't remember something and has to try to think, and perhaps look up, the information a second, third, fourth time until they devise a method to remember or the repetition means the information is stored in the attic, then this effort will pay off in memory. It's a similar principle to the one I mentioned about testing information that has not even been learned yet (earlier in this chapter). You're priming the brain for the information so that there are the 'aha' moments. Answering questions on a topic you know nothing about and getting it all wrong is one of the best ways to learn the correct material. As said, even incorrect recall is better than no recall as long as you look up or find out the right answers in the end. Students will need feedback that corrects any mistakes. (e.g.

Roediger et al., 2010), but not being able to remember or remembering incorrectly and *then* getting corrective feedback helps to encode the information into the memory in the long term.

Optimal Testing Schedules

So, what is the best way to recall?

- The best formula is to recall through an initial short-answer quiz and not through multiple-choice type tests (Kang et al., 2007).
- A key concept for all involved to understand is that the timing of the first test of learning is crucial. Testing immediately after learning some content is simply testing the short-term memory and no effort is required for this. It is too easy to remember the content at this point of the process.

The problem is that learners will think they know the material because they were successful in a test that happened straight after learning (*foresight bias* – see earlier). Therefore, the *timing* of the first test is crucial. Some forgetting of the learned content needs to have occurred so that the remembering is harder (Bjork, 2011; Bjork, 2015; Bjork and Bjork, 2019). Although it is counterintuitive to think this way, it is the forgetting that increases the encoding of the studied material and therefore the memory retains the content much more strongly. It's forgetting and the effort that is needed (e.g. Roediger and Karpicke, 2011).

Two good mantras for your educational setting should be:

1. 'study, test, test, test', and
2. 'forgetting and effort = long-term memory'.

Back to Effort

The reason for this is explained by Whitten and Bjork (1977). They attribute the powerful learning and retention that happens when the first test is delayed and made harder to the memory searching through stored items in the brain to find links, match cues and also the accessing of information in the semantic and acoustic memories.

There are two important benefits to making the first test hard, which is achieved by allowing some forgetting to have set in so allowing a couple of days to elapse after learning the information.

1. To search for the information and find it or be told the information afterwards, once you have searched, strengthens the item's encoding power into the memory. We are not robots, and we cannot simply output information that is input into us. Thus delaying the first test, allowing for forgetting and having to really try to remember 'effortful retrieval', will make the eventual remembering more durable (it will go into the long-term memory rather than the short term); it is learning for life; securing an access place in the 'brain attic'.

2. It is because the retrieval takes more time and is not immediate (as it is if cramming for a test and then recalling straight away). This makes the recall journey more complex; it is slower into memory and creates a more elaborate route into the memory and thus, will be more recallable in the future.

In a Nutshell

The optimal conditions of testing are: effortful recall, and allowing some time to elapse so that forgetting happens. Using the testing effect with interleaving and spacing to create a 'study, test, test, test' model will help to guide your setting to the necessary training for teachers to be able put this into practice with your students for optimal outcomes for all.

It is important to note that while some of the above paragraphs have focused on the benefits and necessities of a schedule like this to support students who suffer with test anxiety, the principles would benefit whole cohorts and not just students who are anxious about taking tests. Research (Weems et al., 2015) recommends the use of 'blanket' interventions in schools, suggesting it is likely all students' wellbeing benefits from such a blanket approach. The suggested PSHE/Pastoral Scheme of Work in Chapter 6 takes you through the training and teaching needed.

Before we look at an optimal schedule for testing - an example, proforma, suggestion - let's consider some scenarios.

1. You are the academic lead in school and a parent has come to visit you because she is concerned that her daughter is not doing enough revision for her upcoming GCSEs. Her mock grades were average and she's saying she can't revise in school when the teachers set revision lessons.
2. As a history teacher, you are concerned by the amount of content you must cover for GCSEs. Already, you offer a lunchtime clinic and before-school session. You attended an INSET on using desirable difficulties and can see the value of testing the students, but you don't have time to 'interleave' and 'space', as they just have to know the content for the exam.
3. You are a form tutor for Year 11. You have been delivering the PSHE/Pastoral Scheme of Work about using desirable difficulties to revise but notice that many of your students believe that real learning is re-reading. Some of the students spend ages highlighting and making revision notes look pretty, but there's really not a lot of recall going on. When you talk to them, they say they prefer blocking/cramming as it's easier and there's a girl on social media who says she got 11 A* from cramming the night before her exams.

Scenario 1: Suggestions for the Academic Lead

- Ask the parent if they attended your 'Desirable difficulties training for parents'. If no, briefly explain and offer to send the resources through, including video links etc.
- Establish how much revision the daughter is doing and how she is doing it. Explain that 60 minutes can be more effective if broken into three chunks of 20 minutes with no phone present and the correct revision materials.
- Provide links to tests, suggest flashcards, ask if mum has time to test and if the daughter can have a friend round to work with or go to a friend to test.
- Establish if mum is using fear appeals or not. Explain the theory around these. If daughter is anxious (she appears so in school) then these appeals could be sending her over the edge.
- Explain that the school has set up recall periods, not study periods, so these should be working but that you will talk to the daughter to find out why she feels she cannot study in school. (Turns out her mates are distracting her – so you may need to re think the study/recall sessions and how they are organized?)
- Go through the grades the daughter is predicted. They are higher than the mock grades. Mum explains that her daughter is just terrified of the whole exam process and will give up rather than face it. Arrange some 1:1/group/tutor time revision of the power of the testing effect and ask the daughter to become an 'exam champion' and to use her social media to (1) design a social media post for the school that teaches about desirable difficulties and the power of this way of learning; and (2) champions positive morning messages all the way through the exam season.
- Talk to mum/daughter about writing strategies ahead of an exam. Practise recall of content in the room the daughter will take the exam.

Scenario 2: Suggestions for the History Teacher

- Talk to your line manager, head of department, person responsible in school for desirable difficulties training.
- Talk to the students about the problem – seek their solutions.
- Consider a general club/extracurricular provision where testing for history could feature.
- Perhaps an ex-student (who loved history) could come in and run retrieval practice sessions for you?
- Think about the possibility of interleaving and testing into a revision (homework) schedule.
- Consider using your assembly duties as retrieval practice sessions.
- You could post quizzes onto the school's social media. Invite students to come up with the quizzes for homework and start running or competition (either you or them).
- Have quizzes on the wall of the lunch hall, the entrance hall, the toilets ('Sorry I'm late miss; I was doing a quiz' – maybe not the toilets!), the history corridor and why not the maths' corridor and office doors. Send quizzes home and ask parents to stick them on fridges.
- Use any extra give in the school calendar to squeeze a history quiz in.

Using Desirable Difficulties to Give Back Control 51

The ideas here are to sideline this out of the main curriculum into some fun quizzing that can take part outside of the class and give you extra time on history in a fun way. Students are really good at coming up with solutions to problems and they'd always be my 'go to' if I wanted to do something to benefit them but couldn't see a way through – they will. So, get the students to create the quizzes on the content for homework and then work out a distribution plan and a way to organize a competition with it.

Scenario 3: Suggestions for the Form Teacher

- Show them the social media example made by another student (see Scenario 1 suggestions) or get them to make a different social media post for the school about using desirable difficulties.
- Role play (with another student/teacher) a scenario where someone has studied using the desirable difficulties and someone has crammed and their feelings on the test morning (although don't do this too near to exams).
- Go over how anxiety-inducing cramming can be.
- Use humour to make a video for the school's media channels of you throwing away all highlighter pens, stamping on them, etc. – to get the point across.
- Make 'study, test, test, test' posters, order stationery with the mantra on, create a competition to get this into conversations with their teachers, peers, parents; create a 'sponsored' how many people can you tell about 'study, test, test, test' in one week competition for a charity. All teachers have to say it 10 times in every lesson or they forfeit a homework ...

The world is your oyster here – there are so many things you can do to get the message across. Have fun! A Worked Example for an Optimal Testing/Revision Schedule

An optimal testing schedule for someone who is taking three A levels may look something like Table 3.2.

By 'input', I suggest reading a section of subject notes or making and using flashcards – some form of 'inputting the information' into memory. If using practice papers – a common theme in my house – don't lose sight of continuing studying and recalling (quizzing) yourself on the actual content of your course.

NB: It's not the amount of time that is spent revising; it's how effective the revision is. These timings are guidelines only. I suggest 45 minutes on input, 30 minutes on recall and 30 minutes checking responses. At weekends, this amount of time could double. Incidentally, it is a neuromyth that music helps concentration and a firm recommendation to leave phones outside or away from the place of study/recall. They're just a distraction. Use them afterwards for looking up anything you couldn't answer.

A further thought: I have not gone into all approaches to learning and all of memory in this chapter – for example, the benefits of dual coding. Other experts offer this and I only have so much room!

Table 3.2 Suggested Optimal Weekly Testing/Revision Schedule Using Interleaving, Spacing and The Testing Effect for A levels

Monday	Input Chemistry 45	Recall using short answer quizzes - Physics* 30	Check answers, correct any mistakes - note anything you need to ask 30
Tuesday	Input Physics 45	Recall using short answer quizzes - Geography* 30	Check answers, correct any mistakes - note anything you need to ask 30
Wednesday	Input Geography 45	Recall using short answer quizzes - Chemistry * 30	Check answers, correct any mistakes - note anything you need to ask 30
Thursday	Input Chemistry 45	Recall using short answer quizzes - Physics* 30	Check answers, correct any mistakes - note anything you need to ask 30
Friday	Input Physics 45	Recall using short answer quizzes - Geography* 30	Check answers, correct any mistakes - note anything you need to ask 30
Saturday	Input Geography 45	Recall using short answer quizzes - Chemistry* 30	Check answers, correct any mistakes - note anything you need to ask 30
Sunday	Input all three subjects 45 x 45 x 45	Recall using short answer quizzes all three subjects* 30 x 30 x 30	Check answers, correct any mistakes - note anything you need to ask 30

Perhaps the movement in this feels counterintuitive to you as an educator and certainly to students. To move onto another topic or subject before completing a topic or subject is unheard of. But massing or cramming information and then testing is blocked practice and it is nowhere near as effective in the long term as interleaving, spacing and testing yourself. It's called 'desirable difficulties' for a reason.

These recall sessions may well take the form of past papers. The important thing is to mix up the recall - to interleave it over a couple of days so that forgetting sets in.

Repeat each week over a period of three to four months. Substitute personal subjects where needed. For GCSEs, the same principle should be adopted but obviously there are more subjects to cover, but input, recall and checking time should be less allowing coverage of two subjects a night.

NB: On occasions, in this book, I have used older academic references. Just a note to say that because they are older does not mean that they are not valid.

Izawa (1970) searched for the number of tests that might produce optimal acquisition of learning and the answer was seven if corrective feedback is given. If feedback is not given, then the total of tests for optimal learning was 19. Izawa's experiments showed that where testing answers are wrong and feedback is provided, the encoding of the learning is powerful.

Feedback is Critical

At the beginning of this book and as part of the whole School Development Plan (Chapter 9), I suggested that your educational setting takes a close look at how feedback, especially after tests, happens in your school or college.

How do you manage peer comparison? How do you get students out of the mindset that tests are to be endured so that they start to look forward to them as learning opportunities – knowing that recall aids recall? How can you ensure that they value and learn from their mistakes?

I suggest here may be cultural changes that need to happen and then embedded in your setting. Think about what your first messages are to students when they join the school. Are they about results? Or are they about learning?

Feedback is a priority in all aspects of education. Kornell, Hays and Bjork (2009) corroborated Izawa's (1970) findings, which were that tests make the learning more powerful when the answer is presented after a test. Marsh, Agarwal and Roediger (2009) suggest that it's vital that feedback is given in circumstances in which it can be carefully processed. If too much peer comparison is dominating the feedback process, individual students may not be absorbing what they need to absorb. Roediger, Agarwal et al. (2010) refer to the direct benefit of testing material for powerful retention in memory and to the issue that feedback of the correct answers improves even more the power of the testing effect or retrieval practice. The feedback is very important when the first test performance is low. In addition, they suggest that multiple tests produce a larger testing effect and short answers, or essay tests produce a better testing effect than multiple choice or true/false options. The key point for educators and students to note is that the short answer is the most effective form of recall at getting the information into the long-term memory.

Yang, Luo et al. (2021) conducted a meta-analysis of the testing effect/retrieval practice and found that feedback that corrects wrong answers worked well because it gives re-exposure to the initial material that has been learned and this results in larger gains in learning. Butler et al. (2008) and Roediger and Marsh (2005) suggest that if students make mistakes on the initial tests and do not receive corrective feedback, it is possible they will make the same mistakes on further tests. Finally, delaying feedback by a couple of days can promote better long-term retention. (e.g. Butler et al., 2008).

Bjork's (1975) idea of recall being a *memory modifier* (retrieval or recall makes it easier to recall) and the significant results from Roediger and Karpicke (2006a,b) about the benefits of 'study, test, test, test' being 150% more effective than either 'study, study, study, test' or 'study, test, study, test, study, test' should underpin a school/educational setting's approach in advising students how to prepare for exams. These principles are fully explored in Chapter 6, which covers the PSHE/Pastoral Scheme of Work that schools can follow for effectively trying to give students back control over taking tests.

I am aware of the ground I have covered in this chapter and so ask you to consider the following key points in summary.

Takeaways

- A school/educational setting, its teachers and students need to know about desirable difficulties research and how this works on memory – this information is in Chapter 6 (which is dedicated to the practical PSHE/Pastoral Scheme of Work) as well as the theoretical guidance and examples in this chapter.
- A school/educational setting needs to know about adopting a metacognition of learning approach alongside teaching desirable difficulties – and to work out the best way for different-aged students in the setting can monitor their learning. Myths about cramming and blocking and judgements of learning need to be exposed, and learning for life habits adopted. The biases of hindsight and foresight should be explicitly taught.
- To ensure all of this, an educational setting will need to do some thinking and auditing around how feedback is managed in school, how teachers are teaching for exams, and especially about how exam feedback is managed. Some suggestions for this can be found in the whole School Development Plan in Chapter 9. These tenets will need to be included in the whole school/college development plan and become embedded within a school culture.
- Teaching students how desirable difficulties work on memory, how recall aids recall, and how this will help in exams helps students anxious about taking tests. It improves their wellbeing and all students may benefit from learning how to learn for life.

Three Soapboxes!

Soapbox 1: *Until there is radical change in the way students are assessed in the UK we will face the problem of anxiety about exams and the issue of cramming (wastefully) for tests.*

Soapbox 2: *So much creativity could be given to the education of our young people. Instead, we 'block' them and test them in subjects they're not even interested in because it has to fit into a GCSEs 'bucket', which the school is then assessed on.*

Soapbox 3: *The time for change in how we assess is long overdue and, given that the wellbeing of our youth is in tatters, it is now imperative that we work for change. It would mean the biggest change education has ever seen. Creative learning for diverse careers that focus on problem-solving and cross-pollination of ideas and learning for life, not end of Key Stage tests.*

Homework

Here are some questions for you to answer on this chapter.

1. Can blocking or cramming ever be good?
2. Why is forgetting knowledge good?
3. What does the phrase 'your testing routes are well-oiled' actually mean?
4. How does the phrase in question 3 help students who are anxious about exams?

5. What different biases have you read about in this chapter? What are they?s
6. Why is metacognition of learning important?
7. What are the 'desirable difficulties' and why are they desirable and difficult?
8. When is the best time for a first test?
9. This is all great in theory but what are some of the issues that educators are up against?
10. What are your own soapbox moments?

Memory Hotspot: Memory Palace the Exam Room

I suggested that a key thing to do may be to take the learning to the room where the high-stakes tests happen and practise using memory palaces in there so that students can picture the content when they walk into the room. For example, the clock by the wall is where all the knowledge on photosynthesis is stored; the door at the side is where the life cycle of worms information is kept; the window on the right is how pollination works! This may really help with test anxiety because you can recall where you have placed the knowledge – actually in the exam room. Word of caution: schools change arrangements – for example, in the event of a fire – but as long as you can picture the hall in your mind's eye, you've got the knowledge.

References and Further Reading

Agarwal, P. K., Roediger, H. L., McDaniel, M. A. & McDermott, K. B. (2010). Improving student learning through the use of classroom quizzes: Three years of evidence from the Columbia Middle School Project (ED513945). *Society for Research on Educational Effectiveness*. ERIC. https://eric.ed.gov/?id=ED513945

Agarwal, P. K., D'Antonio, L., Roediger, H. L., McDermott, K. B. & McDaniel, M. A. (2014). Classroom-based programs of retrieval practice reduce middle school and high school students' test anxiety. *Journal of Applied Research in Memory and Cognition*, 3(3), 131-139. https://doi.org/10.1016/j.jarmac.2014.07.002

Agarwal, P. K., Finley, J. R., Rose, N. S. & Roediger, H. L., 3rd (2017) Benefits from retrieval practice are greater for students with lower working memory capacity, *Memory*, 25(6), 764-771.

Bates, G. & Shea, J. (2024). Retrieval practice 'in the wild': Teachers' reported use of retrieval practice in the classroom. *Mind, Brain, and Education*, 18: 249-257. https://doi.org/10.1111/mbe.12420

Bjork, R. A. (1975). *Retrieval as a memory modifier: An interpretation of negative recency and related phenomena*. In R. L. Solso (ed.), *Information processing and cognition: The Loyola Symposium* (pp. 123-144). Mahwah, NJ: Lawrence Erlbaum. https://bjorklab.psych.ucla.edu/wp-content/uploads/sites/13/2016/07/RBjork_1975.pdf

Bjork, R. A. & Bjork, E. L. (1992). A new theory of disuse and an old theory of stimulus fluctuation. In A. F. Healy, S. M. Kosslyn & R. M. Shiffrin (eds.), *Essays in honor of William K. Estes, Vol. 1. From learning theory to connectionist theory; Vol. 2. From learning processes to cognitive processes* (pp. 35-67). Mahwah, NJ: Lawrence Erlbaum. https://bjorklab.psych.ucla.edu/wp-content/uploads/sites/13/2016/07/RBjork_EBjork_1992.pdf

Bjork, E. L. & Bjork, R. A. (2011). *Making things hard on yourself, but in a good way: Creating desirable difficulties to enhance learning*. In M. A. Gernsbacher, R. W. Pew & J. R. Pomerantz (eds.) & FABBS Foundation, *Psychology and the real world: Essays illustrating fundamental contributions to society* (pp. 56-64). Cheltenham: Worth Publishers. https://bjorklab.psyybch.ucla.edu/wp-content/uploads/sites/13/2016/04/EBjork_RBjork_2011.pdf

Bjork, R. A. (2011). On the symbiosis of remembering and forgetting and learning. In A. S. Benjamin (ed.), *Successful remembering and successful forgetting. A festschrift in honor of Robert A. Bjork* (pp. 1-17). Oxford: Psychology Press, Taylor & Francis Group. https://bjorklab.psych.ucla.edu/wp-content/uploads/sites/13/2016/07/RBjork_2011.pdf

Bjork, R. A. (2015). Forgetting as a friend of learning. In D. S. Lindsay (ed.) & C. M. Kelley (trans.), & A. P. Yonelinas, H. L. Roediger II (eds.), *Psychology Press festschrift series. Remembering: Attributions, processes, and control in human memory: Essays in honor of Larry Jacoby* (pp. 15-28). Oxford: Psychology Press, Taylor & Francis Group. https://bjorklab.psych.ucla.edu/wp-content/uploads/sites/13/2016/11/RABjork_JacobyFestschriftChapterFigsEmbedded052014.pdf

Bjork, R. A. & Bjork, E. L. (2019a). Forgetting as the friend of learning: Implications for teaching and self-regulated learning. *Advances in Physiology Education, 43*(2), 164-167. https://doi.org/10.1152/advan.00001.2019

Bjork, R. A. & Bjork, E. L. (2019b). The myth that blocking one's study or practice by topic or skill enhances learning. In C. Barton (ed.), *Education myths: An evidence-informed guide for teachers*. Melton: John Catt Educational Ltd. https://bjorklab.psych.ucla.edu/wp-content/uploads/sites/13/2020/01/BjorkBjorkEducatinMythChapterPublishedFormSept2019.pdf

Bjork, R. A. & Bjork, E. L. (2020) Desirable difficulties in theory and practice, *Journal of Applied Research in Memory and Cognition, 9*(4), 475-479. UCLA Bjork Learning and Forgetting Lab. https://bjorklab.psych.ucla.edu/wp-content/uploads/sites/13/2021/01/RABjorkELBjorkJARMAC2020ForPostingSingleSpaced.pdf

Bjork, R. A., Dunlosky, J. & Kornell, N. (2013). Self-regulated learning: Beliefs, techniques and illusions. *Annual Review of Psychology, 64*, 417-444. https://doi.org/10.1146/annurev-psych-113011-143823

Brown, P. C., Roediger, H. L., McDaniel & M. A. (2014). *Make it stick: The science of successful learning*. Cambridge, MA: The Belknap Press of Harvard University Press. https://doi.org/10.1080/00220671.2015.1053373

Butler, A. C. & Roediger, H. L. (2007). Testing improves long-term retention in a simulated classroom setting. *European Journal of Cognitive Psychology, 19*(4-5), 514-527. https://doi.org/10.1080/09541440701326097

Butler, A. C., Karpicke, J. D. & Roediger, H. L. (2008). Correcting a metacognitive error: Feedback increases retention of low-confidence correct responses. *Journal of Experimental Psychology: Learning, memory, and cognition, 34*(4), 918-928. https://doi.org/10.1037/0278-7393.34.4.918

Dirkx, K. J. H., Camp, G., Kester, L. & Kirschner, P. A. (2019). Do secondary students make use of effective study strategies when they study on their own? *Applied Cognitive Psychology, 3* (5), 952-957. https://doi.org/10.1002/acp.3584

Dunlosky, J., Rawson, K. A., Marsh, E. J., Nathan, M. J. & Willingham, D. T. (2013). Improving students' learning with effective learning techniques: Promising directions from cognitive and educational psychology. *Psychological Ccience in the Public Interest: A Journal of the American Psychological Society, 14*(1), 4-58. https://doi.org/10.1177/1529100612453266

Fischhoff, B. (1975). Hindsight is not equal to foresight: The effect of outcome knowledge on judgment under uncertainty. *Journal of Experimental Psychology: Human Perception and Performance, 1*(3), 288-299. https://doi.org/10.1037/0096-1523.1.3.288

Giebl, S., Mena, S., Storm, B. C., Bjork, E. L. & Bjork, R. A. (2020). Answer first or Google first? Using the internet in ways that enhance, not impair, one's subsequent retention of needed information. *Psychology Learning & Teaching, 20*(1), 58-75. https://doi.org/10.1177/1475725720961593 (original work published 2021).

Horn, E. & Ashbaugh, E. J. (1920). Lippincott's Horn-Ashbaugh speller for grades 1-8. New York: Lippincott. https://www.gutenberg.org/files/33826/33826-h/33826-h.htm

Imundo, M. N., Pan, S. C., Bjork, E. L. & Bjork, R. A. (2020). Where and how to learn: The interactive benefits of contextual variation, restudying, and retrieval practice for learning. *Quarterly Journal of Experimental Psychology*. https://doi.org/10.1177/1747021820968483

Izawa, C. (1970). Optimal potentiating effects and forgetting-prevention effects of tests in paired associate learning. *Journal of Experimental Psychology, 83*(2, Pt.1), 340-344. https://doi.org/10.1037/h0028541

Kang, S. H., McDermott, K. & Roediger, H. L. (2007). Test format and corrective feedback modify the effect of testing on long-term retention. *European Journal of Cognitive Psychology, 19*, 528-558. https://doi.org/10.1080/09541440601056620

Karpicke, J. D. & Roediger, H. K. (2008). The critical importance of retrieval for learning. *Science, 319*, 966-968. https://doi.org/10.1126/science.1152408

Koriat, A. & Bjork, R. A. (2006a). Illusions of competence during study can be remedied by manipulations that enhance learners' sensitivity to retrieval conditions at test. *Memory & Cognition, 34*(5), 959-972. https://doi.org/10.3758/bf03193244

Koriat, A. & Bjork, R. A. (2006b). Mending metacognitive illusions: A comparison of mnemonic-based and theory-based procedures. *Journal of Experimental Psychology: Learning, Memory and Cognition 2006, 32*(5),1133-1145. https://doi.org/10.1037/0278-7393.32.5.1133

Kornell, N. & Bjork, R. A. (2007). The promise and perils of self-regulated study. *Psychonomic Bulletin & Review, 14*(2), 219-224. https://doi.org/10.3758/BF03194055

Kornell, N., Hays, M. J. & Bjork, R. A. (2009). Unsuccessful retrieval attempts enhdfance subsequent learning. *Journal of Experimental Psychology: Learning, Memory and Cognition, 35*(4), 989-998. https://doi.org/10.1037/a0015729

Kornell, N., Klein, P. J. & Rawson, K. A. (2015). Retrieval attempts enhance learning, but retrieval success (versus failure) does not matter. *Journal of Experimental Psychology: Learning, Memory, and Cognition, 41*(1), 283-294. https://doi.org/10.1037/a0037850

Marsh, E. J., Agarwal, P. K. & Roediger, H. L. III. (2009). Memorial consequences of answering SAT II questions. *Journal of Experimental Psychology: Applied, 15*(1), 1-11. https://doi.org/10.1037/a0014721

Pan, S. C., Bjork & R. A. (2021). Acquiring a mental model of learning: Towards an owner's manual. In A. Wagner and M. Kahana (eds.), *Oxford handbook of learning and memory: Foundations and applications*. Oxford: Oxford University Press.

Pyc, M. A. & Rawson, K. A. (2010). Why testing improves memory: Mediator effectiveness hypothesis. *Science, 330*(6002), 335. https://doi.org/10.1126/science.1191465

Roediger, H. L. & Karpicke J. D. (2006a). The power of testing memory. Basic research and implications for educational practice. *Perspectives on Psychological Science, 1*(3), 181-210. https://doi.org/10.1111/j.1745-6916.2006.00012.x

Roediger, H. L. & Karpicke J. D. (2006b). Test-enhanced learning: Taking memory tests improves long-term retention. *Psychological Science, 17*(3) 249-255. https://doi.org/10.1111%2Fj.1467-9280.2006.01693.x

Roediger, H. L. & Karpicke, J. D. (2011). Intricacies of spaced retrieval: A resolution. In A. S. Benjamin (ed.), *Successful remembering and successful forgetting: Essays in honor of Robert A. Bjork* (pp. 23-48). New York: Psychology Press.

Roediger, H. L. & Marsh, E. J. (2005). The positive and negative consequences of multiple-choice testing. *Journal of experimental psychology. Learning, memory, and cognition, 31*(5), 1155-1159. https://doi.org/10.1037/0278-7393.31.5.1155

Roediger, H. L., Agarwal, P. K., Kang, S. H. K. & Marsh, E.J. (2010). *Benefits of testing memory: Best practices and boundary conditions.* In G. M. Davies & D. B. Wright (eds.), *Current issues in memory. Current issues in applied memory research* (pp.13-49). London: Psychology Press.

Roediger, H. L., Agarwal, P. K., McDaniel, M. A. & McDermott, K. B. (2011). Test-enhanced learning in the classroom: Long-term improvements from quizzing. *Journal of Experimental Psychology: Applied, 17*(4), 382-395. https://doi.org/10.1037/a0026252

Smith, S. M., Glenberg, A. & Bjork, R. A. (1978). Environmental context and human memory. *Memory & Cognition, 6*(4), 342-353. https://doi.org/10.3758/BF03197465

Tsapali, M. (2019). *Effects of different learning environments on late primary school students' decision-making competence in socio-scientific issues* (doctoral thesis). https://doi.org/10.17863/CAM.54222

Weems, C. F., Scott, B. G., Graham, R. A., Banks, D. M., Russell, D. J., Taylor, L. K., Cannon, M. F., Varela, R. E., Scheeringa, M. A., Perry, A. M. and Marino, R. C. (2015). Fitting anxious emotion-focused intervention into the ecology of schools: Results from a test anxiety program evaluation. *Prevention Science, 16*(2), 200-210. https://doi.org/10.1007/s11121-014-0491-1

Whitten, W. B. & Bjork, R. A. (1977). Learning from tests: Effects of spacing. *Journal of Verbal Learning & Verbal Behavior, 16*(4), 465-478.
https://doi.org/10.1016/S0022-5371(77)80040-6

Yang, C., Luo, L., Vadillo, M. A., Yu, R. & Shanks, D. R. (2021). Testing (quizzing) boosts classroom learning: A systematic and meta-analytic review. *Psychological Bulletin*. Advance online publication. https://doi.org/10.1037/bul0000309

4 Self-efficacy in Test-Taking

What to Expect

This is a shorter but important chapter. It gives an introduction to Self-efficacy Theory. It also looks at Confidence Questionnaires and analyses. Additionally, there's information on perceived control, uncertain control and giving back control, plus how test anxiety affects wellbeing.

Key Terms

control: feeling more in control of the testing situation by being able to rely on how you know you have learned reduces worry about taking tests
perceived control: how a student feels about their ability to perform in an exam
uncertain control: the control a student thinks that they have in being able to achieve a successful outcome
wellbeing: in this context, wellbeing around taking exams

We have said we need to give back students, especially anxious students, **control** so they feel more confident in the anxiety-inducing states of taking high-stakes tests. In order to understand this idea fully, it is important to look at the theory of self-efficacy (Bandura, 1997) or belief in capability.

Self-efficacy Theory

Self-efficacy theory (Bandura, 1997) is about an individual's perception of their capability in managing a resulting situation. Zeidner and Matthews (2005) state that self-efficacy is more strongly related to successful performance than is self-esteem.

Repeated here (Figure 4.1) is the test anxiety theory – the transactional model you first encountered in Chapter 1. Self-efficacy theory, the subject of this current chapter, is evident

DOI: 10.4324/9781003534068-4

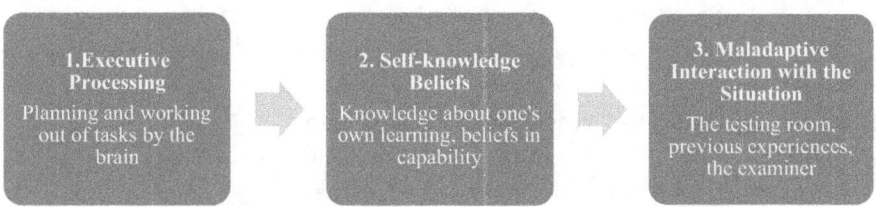

Figure 4.1 The S-REF Model – Self-Referent Executive Function (Zeidner and Matthews, 2005).

in Box 2 of the model: 'Self-knowledge Beliefs – Knowledge about one's own learning, beliefs in capability'.

The intervention, which is the PSHE/Pastoral Scheme of Work, was designed to intervene with students who are anxious about exams at Box 2: Self-knowledge Beliefs. It is at this point that a student who may have trait anxiety and for whom the context of exams is overwhelming starts to imagine the worst, or may recall a previous bad exam experience and start to panic. (As we already know from studying the power of recall, it is easier to see just how powerful a bad memory can be if it is constantly dwelt upon.) Alternatively, a student who suffers with state test anxiety (and may not have as many coping strategies as a trait anxious person – ironically enough) can start to have the fight, flight, freeze thinking. Thus, it becomes necessary to break the pattern here. The PSHE/Pastoral Scheme of Work intervention teaches self-efficacy in test-taking as a means of giving back control to the students when they are taking tests. The questionnaire that follows, 'How Confident Are You?' (see Appendix B at the end of this book for a downloadable version) gives educators the measure that is needed to determine how self-efficacious students feel.

The questionnaire was compiled using Bandura's recommendations for designing questionnaires on self-efficacy (Bandura 2006). One principle is that self-efficacy is domain specific and, in this case, the domain was self-efficacy in test-taking.

Questionnaire to Establish Self-efficacy in Test-Taking: How Confident Are You?

1. = I never do this
2. = I do this sometimes
3. = I do this many times
4. = I always do this

1. If I find a test hard, I keep trying. _____
2. If I find a test hard, I still feel confident in my ability to pass. _____
3. If I did badly on a test, I still feel positive about other tests. _____

4. If I find a test hard, I feel I will not pass. _____
5. When I take tests, I feel anxious about being in a different room to my usual classroom. _____
6. When I take tests, I feel anxious about the instructor. _____
7. If I find a test hard, I can't control negative thoughts about failing. _____
8. If I find a test hard, I start to doubt my ability to pass. _____
9. In tests, I panic if I see people finishing before me. _____
10. I can concentrate in tests, even if I find them difficult. _____
11. I enjoy taking tests. _____
12. I can remain cheerful about life, even if a test is hard. _____
13. I can manage in tests, even if I feel tired or unwell. _____
14. I understand that even if I find a test difficult, it is not the end of the world. _____
15. I don't worry about taking tests. _____

Analysing Responses From the Confidence Questionnaire

Questions 1, 2, 3, 10, 11, 12, 13, 14, 15 with a higher value will indicate someone who does feel confident about taking tests. The other questions (4, 5, 6, 7, 8, 9), if responded to with a higher value, will indicate someone who does not feel confident about taking tests. It will be important to ask students to read the questions carefully. Regardless of the outcomes from the questionnaires, the PSHE/Pastoral Scheme of Work needs to be implemented in a blanket fashion to all students. The nature of the Scheme of Work suggests that most students can benefit in some way from the teaching.

In a Nutshell

This is the point: this research, and especially the intervention that is presented in Chapter 6 as a PSHE/Pastoral Scheme of Work, did benefit the most test-anxious students, but it also contributed to the wellbeing of all.

Weems et al. (2010) call for interventions that can benefit the **wellbeing** of the whole school population and feel that an intervention designed to reduce test anxiety may almost inadvertently contribute to overall student wellbeing in school. Belief in capability or self-efficacy ensures that a student will achieve more, regardless of their knowledge (Bandura, 1997). If they believe they can do it (take the exam and pass) no matter what their knowledge level is, they will achieve more. The reverse is also true, and this is when negative thinking can become a self-fulfilling prophecy.

Self-efficacy theory (Bandura, 1997) is about an individual's perception of their capability in managing a situation – their perception of the control they have over the situation.

Exams take control away from students with their alien and strict rules and the strange, silent rooms. It is necessary to have a foolproof strategy, provided in this book for the first time, to address the issue of test anxiety and to bolster confidence in ability, self-efficacy in test-taking in these circumstances.

For Smith et al. (1990), self-efficacy for test success was more important in predicting a student with test anxiety than cognitive interference and poor study skills.

Belief in capability is the key; it's the mindset that's important.

It is self-efficacy that intervenes to support the idea of how a student feels they have control over a situation. It is human nature to want to control an experience and an outcome – the very nature of testing is rather alien, as not all avenues can be controlled for – least of all the questions that appear on a test paper.

Understanding a Bit More About Control in Testing Situations

Perceived control is how a student feels about their ability to perform in an exam (see Putwain and Aveyard, 2018). Putwain and Aveyard suggest that perceived control, academic buoyancy and test competence can help to control the relationship between worry and cognitive test anxiety, and how a student performs in an exam. They measured the relationship between worry (cognitive thoughts) and perceived control. As worry, or cognitive test anxiety increased, higher perceived control decreased. It is imperative that we support our students by reducing the cognitive anxiety or worry around exams.

Perceived control is different from **uncertain control** but both concepts are important to understand when trying to help students by giving them back control. The idea of uncertain control (e.g. Pekrun, 2006; Putwain and Pescod, 2018) is about the control a student thinks that they have in being able to achieve a successful outcome. They are not sure how their actions or strategies for taking exams will affect the outcome of the whole process and this is linked to test anxiety (Putwain and Aveyard, 2018) So, you can see that uncertain control and perceived control are worming their way into box 2 on the SREF model which is the layer about self-beliefs. It is all about the perception of high stakes' tests being threatening (Putwain and Pescod, 2018). This situation may have transpired from many different sources of trait test anxiety/state test anxiety and/or simply stranger danger or the unknown context room people of an exam.

Uncertain control could be reduced if students were allowed some control over the material being tested. Zeidner (1998) suggests that when individuals are allowed some control over computer-assisted instruction, state anxiety is lowered.

In a Nutshell

Perceived control is how a student feels about their ability to perform in an exam, in other words will they cope with the exam, will they get through it, be able to answer the questions etc. and **uncertain control** is how a student feels about the likelihood of success in an exam.

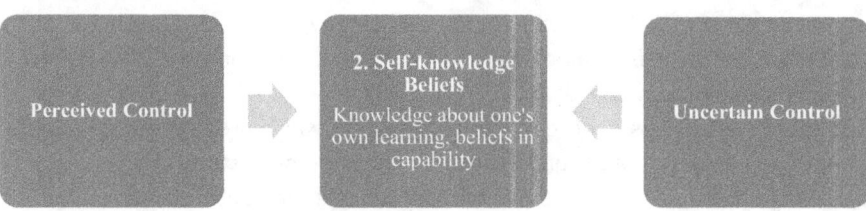

Figure 4.2 Uncertain and Perceived Control, and Box 2.

Putwain, Daly et al. (2015) refer to students' academic buoyancy as being an indicator of how well they will cope in school and with test anxiety. They discuss the relationship between students' self-report levels of test anxiety and academic buoyancy, and suggest training students in the 5Cs of academic buoyancy: confidence, coordination, control, composure and commitment. They suggest a system: individualizing work (differentiation), setting goals, using feedback to reinforce the link between effort and academic outcomes rather than just the outcomes. It is probably fair to say that this system is common practice in many educational settings and differentiation and individual goal setting have been used as good practice in schools since I trained (in 1996). Praise for effort rather than outcome has always been covered in assessment for learning. However, I have included this example here as it may be a useful segway into your own School Development Plan. In particular, the Scheme of Work (see Chapter 6), suggested development plan and teacher training resources in this book focus on arguably the most important two of the Cs – confidence and control – and these are clearly under the self-efficacy umbrella.

Lack of Control in Taking Tests Negatively Affects Wellbeing

Putwain and Pescod (2018) suggest that there is a need for an increase in recognition that test anxiety is associated with poor student wellbeing and it is not simply about test anxiety and performance. For anyone reading this who has had their own child take high-stakes exams, they will hear this sentiment ring true. Households become tense, doors slam, parents wait with bated breath to hear an answer to 'How did it go?' We are talking about young people, whose life chances – e.g. university entry – rest solely on their performance on the day of the exam. Anxiety about exams can mean sleepless nights knowing that there is a need to perform the following day. How many students take their exams with lack of sleep through fear? Surely, we have to question a system that is testing intelligence through a high-stakes test that may produce inaccurate final assessment data? Test-anxious students may not perform to their maximum ability due to a lack of sleep or from fear and anxiety – anxiety about the exam and being unable to recall as they are panicking, and also potentially an ineffective process of revision, driven by the 'blocking' mentality, blocked teaching, fear appeals and trait/state anxiety.

Soapbox: *Why not assess through a series of low-stakes tests where outcomes are not all riding on performance on one day? If a student isn't well (and the likelihood of this increases with anxiety, as it impacts the immune system through over-production of cortisol) how can that be fair? Exam boards may offer 1% of the marks for special consideration. The maximum is about 5%, which as a total amounts to very little. Special consideration from an exam board is hardly ever worth the effort applying. I have seen students take exams when their siblings are dying, a close relative just died, when they are suffering with extreme hay fever, when they are unwell, when they are so anxious they are sick or suffering with migraine. Why are we doing this to young people?*

Getting accurate data about the level of anxiety students feel before an exam is difficult because they are about to take an exam and it is not appropriate to ask them at this point. However, many teachers will know how tense their students are feeling and they too will be waiting with bated breath to see the exam paper, make sure they have taught everything on it, wonder how their students are feeling and how well they will have performed.

While we remain with the current system that uses high stakes tests to determine futures, educators have a moral imperative to try to give students back control so they can do their best in the exams that futures depend on. This is because taking these high-stakes test seriously affects the mental health of many students and arguably their families every year.

Test anxiety poses a risk to wellbeing, particularly vulnerable students (Putwain et al., 2014). These are the students, who are low in academic buoyancy (Putwain et al., 2014). Recently, Putwain et al. (2020) demonstrated that test anxiety is positively correlated to an increase in mental health risk and lowers wellbeing in school. These findings illustrate the potential impact of test anxiety to a student's welfare. If left untreated, it may reduce the wellbeing of students in school (Putwain and Symes, 2018).

Putwain et al. (2021) conclude that there would be benefits to better mental health if test anxiety interventions were used. Weems et al. (2010) suggest that test anxiety interventions in schools can reduce general anxiety and contribute effectively to increasing students' overall wellbeing. In the current ticking time bomb of teenage mental health issues, this has to be a good thing, surely?

More Training?

One of the main issues for schools/educational settings is that not all teachers are routinely trained in supporting mental health issues of students. As the problems that teenagers face become more complex, there is a need for more teacher training in this area. Settings vary. There are some excellent training courses out there and some excellent pastoral teams, but coping with this increase in troubled youngsters and the ever-lengthening waiting lists for proper help means that the increasing expectation to manage complex and numerous mental health issues falls to the teacher, tutor, pastoral team, school, head … anyone who is available!

In a Nutshell

The intervention (PSHE/Pastoral Scheme of Work) is the result of studying test-anxiety literature and the key component of 'the testing effect' from 'desirable difficulties'. Throughout the test-anxiety literature, the inability to recall information when feeling anxious is a constant theme. And, throughout the desirable difficulties literature, the success of recall from testing is a constant theme. This PSHE/Pastoral Scheme of Work is a result of looking at these two theories and realizing that retrieval practice could help with test anxiety but not with the usual subject content recall; instead, it suggests the wellbeing mantra 'your testing routes are well-oiled' in order to increase belief in capability in taking tests.

More Strategies?

In addition to using specific interventions, and particularly the intervention or PSHE/Pastoral Scheme of Work detailed in Chapter 6, some other possible strategies teachers can use to help students include:

- teaching the exam rubric (how papers are set out)
- taking them to the testing room (if possible) and asking them to recall exam content in there
- familiarizing them with how examiners mark.

Most teachers use these strategies already but if you can get your students to regularly recall the information they need for your exam subject in the exam room itself, the impact of doing this could be powerful: it will reduce anxiety because they are used to recalling your subject in the actual exam room where they take the exam, which may reduce anxiety on the day of the exam. This also draws on the idea of using memory palaces (See the Memory Hotspots in Chapters 2 and 3). I have not measured this idea yet (it is further research), but I have spoken to children about this over the years and they like the idea. The Scheme of Work in Chapter 6 is designed to give back control by tackling perceived control and uncertain control.

The PSHE/Pastoral Scheme of Work in the next chapter aims to provide educational settings with the tools they need to help increase feelings of self-efficacy in test-taking for

Figure 4.3 Problem to Solution and Outcome.

students. However, this Scheme of Work should be delivered in conjunction with a whole school or setting rethink about exams covering:

1. how feedback around tests is being managed, and
2. generally, the wellbeing of students around test-taking, which is why a suggested whole School Development Plan is also included (see Chapter 9).

SCENARIOS

The following scenarios may help you to think through some of the complexities covered in this chapter.

1. *You are the SENCo for a small secondary school. You have very limited space and resources for providing access arrangements for all the students who need them. This year is exceptional with the number of students who have anxiety, particularly anxiety around exams. You welcome the new PSHE/Pastoral Scheme of Work that the school has committed to. Not only does it benefit the students, you can tell parents that the school is intervening for all students who are anxious about exams. How would you maximize the impact of this research and how do you deal with the logistics you are facing?*
2. *Kiran is a 'school refuser'. Since COVID-19, she refuses to come into school. At the moment, you are sending work home and visiting once a week to check on her wellbeing/safeguarding. It's year 11 and the GCSEs are looming. Her parents want her to take the exams and are asking you for advice.*
3. *As head of a school, you are interested in this research and can see how it might give confidence to students around tests. What are your pros and cons in rolling out this initiative?*

Scenario 1: Suggestions for the SENCo

As SENCo, you can see the Scheme of Work (Chapter 6) will benefit a full range of students. You ask for this initiative to be itemized on the Senior Management Team agenda as you would like to ensure there is a rolling programme of the intervention in the school calendar to cover all age groups. This would mean that by the time students are reaching Y10, they will have been through a different (differentiated by year group) version of the intervention at least twice if not three times. You have also read the suggestions for a whole School Development Plan (Chapter 9), and with your SENCo hat on, you would like to contribute to 'little things' the school can do to support the wellbeing of students, especially around exams. Your door is always open and, at exam times, stressed pupils are like a drip feed in and out.

You have your eye on some students in particular and you check with those parents if they understood the desirable difficulties training at the beginning of the school year. You offer to support them further in revision strategies for their children by revisiting the training or pointing them in the direction of this book or a student guide aimed at student age groups called 'Manage Test Anxiety'.

You get your SEN students as involved as you can in promoting positive messages about testing. Some schools issue a SEND newsletter. You could use this to feature the Scheme of Work and its benefits for all students. You find a 'desirable difficulty' champion on your team to promote the key ideas.

While moving and supporting the school in these ways, the logistics you face are so tricky this summer; you're having sleepless nights. You need to meet with the Head well ahead of the curve to ensure the required access needs are met for exams – including the mocks – and have your copy of the JCQ regulations with you (as well as your SEND policy); the Head should be familiar with both of these documents.

Scenario 2: Suggestions for Kiran's teacher

OK – tricky. GCSE exams have to be taken at an approved centre. Kiran knows this. She has also been studying and wants to take her exams. On one of the home visits – ahead of the curve – ask how she can take the exam at school or another centre? (You have already subtly found a few places that might be flexible to this request.) You could offer visits to the school and the room where she can take her exam – out of school hours. You can ensure she knows who will be with her in the exam (if she prefers to take them in a separate room). It is important to prepare the ground and ensure that what you say you will do happens on the day. You are clear about what the options are – what you can and cannot do. It has to be an exam centre. It can be school with special access arrangements. There needs to be a continuous adult here – someone who visits Kiran, could be with her and ensures efficiency of process.

Scenario 3: Suggestions for the head

Pros

- Cutting-edge research that benefits all students, and gives staff new knowledge.
- Test-anxious students will really benefit.
- Happy students; happy parents.
- Resources are inexpensive and ready to go with minimum effort.
- It's so much more than a Scheme of Work; it's creating skills for learning for life.
- Students Wellbeing has really taken a hit and this is an opportunity to tangibly do something, plus the knowledge is useful for all teachers – new and old.
- It's a good opportunity to review current practice around testing and feedback.
- It's a good opportunity to combine pastoral, teaching and learning in one initiative and to give staff and students great teaching and learning strategies.

- Great for developing particular members of staff – could be part of an NPQSL (National Professional Qualification for Senior Leadership) and/or NPQH (National Professional Qualification for Headship).
- Positive marketing for the school.

Cons

- You need to give someone time to get their head around this and be able to deliver INSET to parents and staff.
- You need to calendarize the parents' training, the staff training and the year group roll-outs, plus your SENCo is really pushing you to get on top of this! Administrative tasks.
- Skills for learning for life aren't accredited by exam boards and you haven't got time – it's only the grades that matter – in many peoples' eyes.

I'm sure you can keep going here but, on balance, there have to be more pros than cons; anything that benefits students, staff and parents has to be worth it.

Takeaways

- This chapter is about control or a student's lack of control when it comes to taking tests: not knowing the exam questions, not knowing how they will perform, not knowing the invigilator, not knowing the content (if they didn't test themselves), simply the not knowing.
- Self-efficacy theory is domain specific and, in this case, it is self-efficacy in taking tests. A belief in capability in being able to take tests.
- The intervention teaches students about desirable difficulties so they understand how memory works and thereby have more control over their test-taking abilities.

Homework

Now that you have read this chapter, have a think about your answers to these questions. As with all homework questions throughout the book, keep a note of your thoughts or even set up a discussion group with others who are working through this book at the same time as you.

1. What is the difference between perceived control and uncertain control?
2. Apart from delivering the intervention, what else can teachers and schools do to help reduce test anxiety?
3. What is self-efficacy theory?
4. How is self-efficacy being used in the intervention?
5. What issues is your educational setting facing around student wellbeing? Are there other ways that this intervention might help student wellbeing?

Memory Hotspot: Ancient Memory – Quintilian

This whole idea of remembering a place is very old. Simonides of Ceos is credited for remembering who was alive after the roof fell in at a dinner party by using this method of 'loci', or mentally placing information in the brain by position. Quintilian, an educator in Rome, wrote about memory in his treatise *Institutes of Oratory*. He acknowledges that Simonides was the first to teach the 'Art of Memory' (11.2) and that Simonides could recall who was sitting at the party (and therefore who was alive and dead after the roof collapsed) through being 'assisted by localities impressed on the mind'. He goes onto explain how the system of loci works (11.2.18-19):

> People fix in their minds places of the greatest possible extent, diversified by considerable variety, such as a large house, for example, divided into many apartments. Whatever is remarkable in it is carefully impressed on the mind so that the thought may run over every part of it without hesitation or delay ... then (11.2.19) they distinguish what they have written or treasured in their mind by some symbol by which they may be reminded of it, a symbol which may have reference to the subject in general, as navigation or warfare, or to some particular word, for if they forget, they may, by hint from a single word, find their recollection revived.

In a Nutshell

Quintilian's own opinion of memory is that 'it is strengthened, like all our other faculties, by exercise'. This is the equivalent of what we now know about neural plasticity and recall aiding recall!

The idea of growth mindset (Dweck, 2008) is also evident in Quintilian in that using the brain or exercising it can make memory stronger. And Hattie et al.'s chunking of ideas to help memory (2014) is summed up effectively by Quintilian in 11.2.27 by saying 'if a long speech is to be retained in memory, it will be of advantage to learn it in parts, for the memory sinks under a vast burden laid on it at once.'

And the idea that forgetting is also good for memory is touched on in 11.2. 43:

> It is astonishing how much strength of interval the night gives it and a reason for the fact cannot easily be discovered ... It is certain that what could not be repeated at first is readily put together on the following day and the very time which is generally thought to cause forgetfulness is found to strengthen the memory.

And with reference to the downfalls of blocking or massed practice: 11.44: 'On the other hand, the extraordinarily quick memory soon allows what his has grasped to escape it, and as if, after discharging a present duty, it owed nothing further, it resigns its charge like a dismissed steward'.

And with reference to long-term memory: 'Nor is it indeed surprising that what has been longest impressed upon the mind should adhere to it with the greatest tenacity' (Quintillian, 11.2.44), so *there is the ancient vote for retrieval practice*

It's also fascinating that ancient Rome had its own version of memory athletes (11.2.50–51):

> As exemplified by Themistocles who is generally believed to have learned to speak the Persian language accurately in less than a year; or Mithridates, who is said to have known twenty-two languages, one for each of the nations over which he ruled ... Crassus was so well acquainted with the five dialects of the Greek tongue, Cyrus, who is supposed to have known the names of every one of his soldiers. Theodectes, also, is said to have been able to repeat instantly any number of verses after having once hear them. (Quintillian, 11.2.50)

References and Further Reading

Bandura, A. (1997). *Self-efficacy: The exercise of control.* Stanford University, CA: W. H. Freeman/Times Books/Henry Holt & Co.

Bandura, A. (2006). Guide for constructing self-efficacy scales in F. Pajares & T. Urdan (eds.), *Self-efficacy beliefs of adolescents, 5* (pp. 307–337). Information Age Publishing.

Dweck, C. S. (2008). *Mindset: The new psychology of success.* New York: Ballantine Books.

Hattie, J., Yates, G. (2014). *Visible learning and the science of how we learn.* London and New York: Routledge.

Pekrun, R. (2006). The control-value theory of achievement emotions: Assumptions, corollaries, and implications for educational research and practice. *Educational Psychology Review, 18*(4), 315–341. https://doi.org/10.1007/s10648-006-9029-9

Putwain, D. W. (2020). *Examination pressures on children and young people: Are they taken seriously enough? A provocation paper.* The British Academy. https://medium.com/reframing-childhood-past-and-present/examination-pressures-on-children-and-young-people-are-they-taken-seriously-enough-e274b9595d4

Putwain, D. W. & Aveyard, B. (2018). Is perceived control a critical factor in understanding the negative relationship between cognitive test anxiety and examination performance? *School Psychology Quarterly, 33*(1), 65–74. Advance online publication. https://doi.org/10.1037/spq0000183

Putwain, D. W., Chamberlain, S., Daly, A. L. & Sadreddini, S. (2014). Reducing test anxiety among school-aged adolescents: A field experiment. *Educational Psychology in Practice, 30*(4), 420–444, https://doi.org/10.1080/02667363.2014.964392

Putwain, D. W., Daly & A. L. (2014) Test anxiety prevalence and gender differences in a sample of English secondary school students. *Educational Studies, 40*(5), 554–570. https://doi.org/10.1080/03055698.2014.953914

Putwain, D. W. & Pescod, M. (2018). Is reducing uncertain control the key to successful test anxiety intervention for secondary school students? Findings from a randomized control trial. *School Psychology Quarterly, 33*(2), 283–292. https://doi.org/10.1037/spq0000228

Putwain, D. W. & Symes, W. (2018). Does increased effort compensate for performance debilitating test anxiety? *School Psychology Quarterly.* https://psycnet.apa.org/doi/10.1037/spq0000236

Putwain, D. W., Daly, A. L., Chamberlain, S. & Sadreddini, S. (2015). Academically buoyant students are less anxious about and perform better in high-stakes examinations. *The British Journal of Educational Psychology, 85*(3), 247–263. https://doi.org/10.1111/bjep.12068

Putwain, D. W., Gallard, D.C., Beaumont, J., Loderer, K. & von der Embse, N. (2021). Does test anxiety predispose poor school-related wellbeing and enhanced risk of emotion disorders? *Cognitive Therapy and Research.* LJMU Research online. https://researchonline.ljmu.ac.uk/id/eprint/14279/

Quintilian's Institutes of Oratory (n.d.) Edited by Lee Honeycutt; translated by John Selby Watson. Creative Commons License: Attribution NonCommercial ShareAlike 3.0 ISBN: 13:978-1500342661.

Smith, R. J., Arnkoff, D. B. & Wright, T. L. (1990). Test anxiety and academic competence: A comparison of alternative models. *Journal of Counseling Psychology, 37*(3), 313–321. https://doi.org/10.1037/0022-0167.37.3.313

Weems, C. F., Scott, B. G., Taylor, L. K., Cannon, M. F., Romano, D. M., Perry, A. M. & Triplett, V. (2010). Test anxiety prevention and intervention programs in schools: Program development and rationale. *School Mental Health: A Multidisciplinary Research and Practice Journal, 2*(2), 62–71. https://doi.org/10.1007/s12310-010-9032-7

Zeidner, M. (1998) *Test anxiety: The state of the art*. New York: Springer Science+Business.

Zeidner, M. & Matthews, G. (2005). Evaluation anxiety. Current theory and research. In A. J. Elliot & C. S. Dweck (eds.), *Handbook of competence and motivation* (pp. 141–160) London, New York: The Guildford Press.

5 Intervening in Test Anxiety

> **What to Expect**
>
> This chapter covers the intervention itself, the lack of interventions in schools and the need for them in schools. It looks at why writing about exams works, why testing works and how not cramming or blocking makes you less anxious. It examines how recall aids recall and discusses the brain as a muscle. In addition, it looks briefly at teacher-student relationships, plus the idea of students using positive messaging.

> **Key Terms**
>
> **blanket intervention:** everyone benefits
> **brain plasticity:** the amazing things you can do to 're-wire' how you think
> **intervention:** lack of research, lack of interventions; the pressing need for them
> **low working memory:** retrieval practice works with this need
> **recall aids recall:** each time you remember makes it easier to remember again
> **student-teacher relationships:** a book in itself (despite the necessarily brief comment here); experience says it's so important
> **why:** giving students the 'why' of how memory works for tests

The **intervention** PSHE/Pastoral Scheme of Work (fully presented in Chapter 6) is a result of research I carried out between 2016 and 2021. There is still a need for test-anxiety interventions with school-aged populations (see Putwain and Symes, 2018). Putwain (2020, p. 6) refers to a 'pressing need' for a test-anxiety intervention for the primary year group Year 6 (10-11-year-olds). This book, and the intervention – which I have called PSHE/Pastoral Scheme of Work – may contribute to filling that void.

Lack of Research And Intervention

My research demonstrated that an intervention that focuses on the cognitive or worry aspect of test anxiety can be effective at reducing worry about exams. Overall, there is a lack of research into the effectiveness of interventions. There is a lack of research into the effectiveness of test-anxiety programmes for school-aged students. (e.g. Ergene, 2003). The evidence base for school-based intervention programmes is extremely limited. School-based interventions have the potential to lessen or even prevent educational underachievement and the threat to wellbeing that can be the result for students who are high in test anxiety, as a result of possessing low academic buoyancy, low self-efficacy (Weems et al., 2010, 2015). There is a real lack of in-school research and research with school-age groups into using cognitive science, desirable difficulties, the testing effect to reduce test anxiety. Most research around test anxiety and retrieval practice tends to be with undergraduates and psychology students and is often either test-anxiety research or retrieval-practice research.

The intervention was piloted, then a fully tested, researched and evaluated experiment was conducted in schools and the effectiveness of the intervention measured using a quantitative analysis. The results were positive for all students but especially those who were scored highly for test anxiety on the questionnaires. The intervention, as said, has become the Scheme of Work in Chapter 6, and it is hoped that your educational setting will benefit from this. This Scheme of Work can be differentiated further according to need, so that it can be used on all age groups (from 10 years through to 21 years as an estimate). I have tailored the Scheme of Work and its resources to different age groups.

Self-esteem, self-efficacy and cognitive control are key ideas to bear in mind when designing an intervention that will work to give back control and reduce test anxiety when taking exams. In my research, I looked at how a state of mind, a state of anxiety, can be altered by an intervention that uses cognitive theory. The plasticity of the brain (**brain plasticity**) and the ability to change thinking is not a new concept. By manipulating beliefs about self-efficacy in test-taking, we were able to give back some control so that feelings about self-efficacy in test-taking were improved. This was especially true for students who experienced high-test anxiety.

Performance and Reducing Cognitive Test Anxiety

Putwain and Aveyard (2018) focus on how three self-beliefs – academic buoyancy, perceived control and test competence – and how these concepts affect the relationship between worry and test performance. The conclusion is that self-belief might alter the problem of cognitive test anxiety and examination performance.

In a Nutshell

Putwain and Aveyard (2018) suggest that interventions that reduce worry, the cognitive element of test anxiety, can improve an individual's belief in their self-control and their ability to manage the evaluative situation. This is giving back control.

As I have touched on previously, the reason we should conduct the intervention in a blanket **(blanket intervention)** fashion – that is, intervene with all students and not just those who are registering more highly in the questionnaires – is simply explained by Weems et al. (2015). They support the idea of the importance of intervening in test anxiety by applying a universal intervention to improve overall wellbeing. The authors suggest that by lessening the anxiety around evaluative situations through effective interventions, students will achieve more and therefore feel more confident about their results, thus becoming more self-efficacious. Thus, the intervention – or PSHE/Pastoral Scheme of Work – may benefit the wellbeing of all students. The principle is that all students can benefit from support. A universal intervention means that individuals are not at any risk of becoming the focus of unwarranted attention from peers.

> **Nitty Gritty**
>
> The intervention, or the PSHE/Pastoral Scheme of Work, was designed to teach students about the testing effect to give them the 'why' testing works. Giving students the 'why' gives them more control, and students who have high control should have access to more positive self-beliefs and therefore lower worry or cognitive test anxiety (Putwain and Aveyard, 2018).

Using the Testing Effect or Retrieval Practice to Reduce Test Anxiety: Getting Ready to Deliver the Intervention

The intervention is the result of research into test anxiety that identified a layer of thinking/believing that was ripe for intervention. The self-knowledge beliefs layer of the test anxiety S-REF model (Zeidner and Matthews, 2005). In designing the intervention, the ideas were to couple test-anxiety research with the results from the literature that reports the profoundly successful results of desirable difficulties, particularly the testing effect or retrieval practice for retaining information in the long-term memory (Bjork and Bjork, 2011; Roediger and Karpicke 2006a, 2006b; Karpicke and Roediger, 2008). When these ideas merged, it began to feel like a possible solution to the problem of test anxiety. Underpinning all of these ideas and the bedrock of the intervention (Scheme of Work) is self-efficacy theory or belief in capability – in this case, in taking tests.

Agarwal et al. (2014) state that 92% of students feel retrieval practice benefits learning and, importantly, that 72% of students felt that retrieval practice helped them with test anxiety. Retrieval practice has been shown to improve recall for students with **low working memory** (Agarwal et al., 2017). This suggests it is an inclusive strategy for students with this individual need.

The research that has resulted in this book took a different approach. It did not involve taking low stakes-tests on different curricula subject content for different subjects. We took a recall of a wellbeing strategy approach. Using retrieval practice to recall a positive mantra, we asked the students to recall the benefits of using the 'testing effect'.

Benefit 1: Information learned through testing and spacing this out rather than cramming means you have ready access to the information, even when feeling anxious.

Benefit 2: Every time you recall (especially if it's hard to remember), it makes it easier next time to remember. **Recall aids recall**. The research was prompted by students who were about to take high-stakes tests and who were crumbling at the thought of them. So, we taught them about the testing effect or retrieval practice and how the brain works.

Benefit 3: Rather than retrieving the content needed for a test, though, a pastoral retrieval practice approach was adopted. We used retrieval practice of the benefits of retrieval practice. The aim was to get students to understand the principles of retrieval practice (recall aids recall), so that even if the brain is in flight, fight, freeze mode, which is the state of anxiety many students find themselves in before an exam, they can draw on this safe knowledge: 'We have revised by testing ourselves. This means that we do know the material.' The phrase we constantly repeated to the students throughout was: 'Your testing routes are well-oiled."

In a Nutshell

The reason that recall aids recall is that every time you try to remember, you are increasing the strength of the myelin layers in the brain. So, I like to think of this as adding cells to the white stretchy bits in my head. As I struggle to remember, I'm coating those myelin layers with extra cells, extra strength, so it will be easier to remember next time – like working a muscle. That might not be the exact science but it's along those lines. Just think of your brain working out when you're trying to remember; it's good for it, and the more you use those remembering muscles, the easier it becomes to remember.

The results from both the pilot and the main study suggested that the intervention worked. It worked especially well for students who were recording the highest scores on the questionnaire about feeling anxious (see Chapter 4 and the Appendices). That intervention is presented to you in the next chapter as a PSHE/Pastoral Scheme of Work and in a way that it is hoped you can use directly in schools or your educational setting. It takes about 20-30 minutes a week to deliver.

In a Nutshell

Every time a student recalls information, as long as some forgetting has happened and there is effortful retrieval of information, the repeated testing will ensure that knowledge will be retained in the long-term memory and easily accessible for exams. Information will be stored in the brain attic but is accessible! The hope is that knowing how memory works, students will feel more self-efficacious about their test taking abilities.

Student-Teacher Relationships

The relationship between a student and their teacher is a critical one. I know this as a teacher, as a head and mostly as a mum! This intervention/Scheme of Work is a pastoral retrieval practice strategy that should be delivered by someone who cares about the content of this book; someone who is caring for students' pastoral wellbeing. In most cases, this might be the form tutor who has the daily, pastoral knowledge of their students. But it doesn't have to be. The Scheme of Work could be delivered by anyone who has an interest in helping students manage anxiety about tests by giving them more control and is happy to research desirable difficulties. If training several teachers on this is difficult (see Chapters 3 and 8 for training teacher material), it might makes sense to train one or two people (have someone in reserve, too, for when cover is needed) to cover all the year groups.

Writing Tasks As Part of the Intervention

A key element of the intervention/Scheme of Work is writing about retrieval practice, and it might be useful to share the reasons why these tasks have been included in the intervention. Ramirez and Beilock (2001) found that writing about testing worries boosts exam performance. McKeachie (1951) found that anxious students achieved more on multiple-choice questions, taken in exams, if they were allowed to write comments about the questions. McKeachie (1951) described the opportunity as being able to lose or direct some of the tensions created by tests. Two of the tasks in the six-week intervention/Scheme of Work involve writing. There is a reason for this. The idea of writing down worrisome thoughts as a coping strategy for test anxiety is not new (e.g. McKeachie, 1951). Lang and Lang (2010) suggest that boosting confidence through writing positive affirmations ahead of an exam is beneficial for students who are high in test anxiety and improves test-taking self-efficacy. Shen, Lang et al. (2018) suggested that positive writing ahead of taking a test benefited Chinese students. Ramirez and Beilock (2011) found that writing about testing helped students who were high in test anxiety.

Yeager et al. (2013) use the idea of the brain's plasticity and malleability to promote growth mindset about issues such as bullying and aggression in 14-16-year-olds. In this study, the students complete a writing assignment that emphasizes using positive coping skills and avoiding negative coping skills.

The idea of journalling or writing down worries is not a new one and there is a sense of release of the worry once it is out of the brain and on paper. However, in this intervention, we're not asking students to write down worries but note the positive things they have learned about how they study. It's another way of recalling the positive information that we are teaching them about how their memories work and how the brain learns.

> ### In A Nutshell
>
> Writing about the testing effect in a 'Letter to Bob' to allay Bob's fears about the way students learn and writing a letter to a friend to give advice when they are worried about taking tests are the writing activities in the PSHE/Pastoral Scheme of Work – see Chapter 6.

Positive Messages

It may be sensible to advise the students that they can 'do a McKeachie' in the exam (on some scrap paper) with notes about questions – if they find that helpful. Another strategy would be to write positive messages to themselves or others (via social media) before the exam. Rather than the usual 'I'm scared' conversations, if students sent each other positive messages – 'We've been testing; we know this' – it could help them all. Note the suggestion for using student leadership positions of being a positive exam role model.

> **Nitty Gritty**
>
> To my knowledge, the research that I undertook is the first of its kind to use retrieval practice of the testing effect to create self-efficacy in test-taking and reduce test anxiety (Barsham & Ellefson, 2020).

The research was successful in reducing test anxiety, especially with the most anxious students. It is recommended that the intervention that has now been turned into a PSHE/Pastoral Scheme of Work is delivered to all students as it is likely that all will benefit.

Benefits of the Intervention

One real problem for students who have test anxiety is that for some of them test anxiety is a state (Spielberger and Vagg, 1995) that happens as result of the knowledge of the test and thus may not be diagnosed and catered for ahead of the test itself. This is one reason why, in my opinion, universal interventions are a good way to manage test anxiety – hence this book, the practical strategies and PSHE/Pastoral Scheme of Work offered should be delivered to all.

Access Arrangements

Access arrangements for exams mean that some students with individual needs do receive different support. For example, extra time can be awarded or the support of a reader or scribe is offered. Some students with general and test anxiety do have different access arrangements for high stakes' tests. This may take the form of an individual room.

Alternatively, an effective means of diagnosing test anxiety is needed (Putwain et al., 2020; von der Embse et al., 2018) so that appropriate arrangements can be made for taking high-stake tests.

Takeaways

- Writing positive messages can help to reduce test anxiety; the intervention has two writing tasks.

- Everyone can benefit from the intervention.
- The intervention works.
- This is retrieval practice of a wellbeing message about self-efficacy in test taking.
- PSHE/Pastoral Scheme of Work gives student the reason 'why'; it shows them how to revise and how this method of revision works for tests.

Homework

Once you have read this chapter, make a note of your answers to these questions.

1. Does retrieval practice work with low working memory?
2. Why do you think writing positive messages works?
3. How might student-teacher relationships affect a student with test anxiety?
4. Is it important to teach students why retrieval practice works for exams – why?
5. Why should all school-based intervention be delivered in a 'blanket' fashion?
6. Why does recall aid recall?

Memory Hotspot: Hattie's Chunks and CRIME

Educator and author John Hattie (Hattie and Yates, 2014) advocates that we commit a CRIME – a mnemonic in itself:

- **C**hunking information together
- **R**etrieving it (study, test, test, test)
- using **I**magery
- using **M**nemonics such as 'one collar two short sleeves for the spelling of necessary', and
- **E**laboration – anything that will add flair or memorability to the content to be learned like making a mistake.

Hattie also discussed the amount of information that can be held in working memory, and as cognitive scientists we know that we should concentrate on getting people to remember three things if we're speaking.

References and Further Reading

Agarwal, P. K., Finley, J. R., Rose, N. S. & Roediger, H. L., 3rd (2017). Benefits from retrieval practice are greater for students with lower working memory capacity. *Memory* 25(6), 764–771. https://doi.org/10.1080/09658211.2016.1220579

Agarwal, P. K., Roediger, H. L., McDaniel, M. A. & McDermott, K. B. (2010). Improving student learning through the use of classroom quizzes: Three years of evidence from the Columbia Middle School Project. (ED513945) *Society for Research on Educational Effectiveness*. ERIC. https://eric.ed.gov/?id=ED513945

Agarwal, P. K., D'Antonio, L., Roediger, H. L., McDermott, K. B. & McDaniel, M. A. (2014). Classroom-based programs of retrieval practice reduce middle school and high school students' test anxiety.

Journal of Applied Research in Memory and Cognition, 3(3), 131-139. https://doi.org/10.1016/j.jarmac.2014.07.002

Barsham, H. (2021). Can retrieval practice of the testing effect increase self- efficacy in tests and reduce test anxiety in 10- to 11-year-olds? https://www.repository.cam.ac.uk/handle/1810/330201

Barsham, H. & Ellefson, M. R. (2020). Can teaching upper primary about the testing effect increase feelings of confidence about test taking? *Journal of the Chartered College of Teachers, Impact 8.*

Bjork, E. L. & Bjork, R. A. (2011). *Making things hard on yourself, but in a good way: Creating desirable difficulties to enhance learning.* In M. A. Gernsbacher, R. W. Pew & J. R. Pomerantz (eds.) & FABBS Foundation, *Psychology and the real world: Essays illustrating fundamental contributions to society* (pp. 56-64). Cheltenham: Worth Publishers. https://bjorklab.psyybch.ucla.edu/wp-content/uploads/sites/13/2016/04/EBjork_RBjork_2011.pdf

Ergene, T. (2003). Effective interventions on test anxiety reduction. A meta-analysis. *School Psychology International, 24*, 313-328. https://doi.org/10.1177/01430343030243004

Hattie, J. & Yates, G. (2014). *Visible learning and the science of how we learn.* London and New York: Routledge

Karpicke, J. D. & Roediger, H. K. (2008). The critical importance of retrieval for learning. *Science, 319*, 966-968. https://doi.org/10.1126/science.1152408

Lang, J. W. B. & Lang, J. (2010). Priming competence diminishes the link between cognitive test anxiety and test performance: Implications for the interpretation of test scores. *Psychological Science, 21*(6), 811-819. https://doi.org/10.1177/0956797610369492

McKeachie, W. J. (1951). Anxiety in the college classroom. *The Journal of Educational Research, 45*, 153-160.

Putwain, D. W. (2020). *Examination pressures on children and young people: Are they taken seriously enough? A provocation paper.* The British Academy. https://medium.com/reframing-childhood-past-and-present/examination-pressures-on-children-and-young-people-are-they-taken-seriously-enough-e274b9595d4

Putwain, D. W. & Aveyard, B. (2018). Is perceived control a critical factor in understanding the negative relationship between cognitive test anxiety and examination performance? *School Psychology Quarterly, 33*(1), pp 65-74. Advance online publication. https://doi.org/10.1037/spq0000183

Putwain, D. W. & Symes, W. (2018). Does increased effort compensate for performance debilitating test anxiety? *School Psychology Quarterly.* https://psycnet.apa.org/doi/10.1037/spq0000236

Putwain, D. W., von der Embse, N. P., Rainbird, E. C. & West, G. (2020). The development and validation of a new Multidimensional Test Anxiety Scale (MTAS). *European Journal of Psychological Assessment.* Advance online publication. https://doi.org/10.1027/1015-5759/a000604

Ramirez, G. & Beilock, S. L. (2011). Writing about testing worries boosts exam performance in the classroom. *Science (New York, N.Y.), 331*(6014), 211-213. https://doi.org/10.1126/science.1199427

Roediger, H. L. & Karpicke J. D. (2006a). The power of testing memory. Basic research and implications for educational practice. *Perspectives on Psychological Science, 1*(3), 181-210. https://doi.org/10.1111/j.1745-6916.2006.00012.x

Roediger, H. L. & Karpicke J. D. (2006b). Test-enhanced learning: Taking memory tests improves long-term retention. *Psychological Science, 17*(3) 249-255. https://doi.org/10.1111%2Fj.1467-9280.2006.01693.x

Shen. L., Yang, L., Zhang, J. & Zhang, M. (2018). Benefits of expressive writing in reducing test anxiety: A randomized controlled trial in Chinese samples. *PLoS One, (13)*2, 1-15. https://pmc.ncbi.nlm.nih.gov/articles/PMC5798770/pdf/pone.0191779.pdf

Spielberger, C. D. & Vagg, P. R. (1995). Test anxiety. A transactional process model. In C. D. Spielberger & P. R. Vagg (eds.), *Test anxiety, theory, assessment and treatment* (pp. 3-14). London and New York: Taylor & Francis.

von der Embse, N., Jester, D., Devlina, R., Post, J. (2018). Test anxiety effects, predictors, and correlates: A 30-year meta-analytic review. *Journal of Affective Disorders, 227*, 483-493. https://doi.org/10.1016/j.jad.2017.11.048

Weems, C. F., Scott, B. G., Graham, R. A., Banks, D. M., Russell, D. J., Taylor, L. K., Cannon, M. F., Varela, R. E., Scheeringa, M. A., Perry, A. M. & Marino, R. C. (2015). Fitting anxious emotion-focused intervention into the ecology of schools: Results from a test anxiety program evaluation. *Prevention Science, 16*(2), 200-210. https://doi.org/10.1007/s11121-014-0491-1

Weems, C. F., Scott, B. G., Taylor, L. K., Cannon, M. F., Romano, D. M., Perry, A. M. & Triplett, V. (2010). Test anxiety prevention and intervention programs in schools: Program development and rationale. *School Mental Health: A Multidisciplinary Research and Practice Journal, 2*(2), 62-71. https://doi.org/10.1007/s12310-010-9032-7

Yeager, D. S., Trzesniewski, K. H. & Dweck, C. S. (2013). An implicit theories of personality intervention reduces adolescent aggression in response to victimization and exclusion. *Child Development, 84*(3), 970-988. https://doi.org/10.1111/cdev.12003

Zeidner, M. & Matthews, G. (2005). Evaluation anxiety. Current theory and research. In A. J. Elliot & C. S. Dweck (eds.), *Handbook of competence and motivation* (pp. 141-160) London, New York: The Guildford Press.

6 The Intervention
Giving Back Control – Reducing Test Anxiety – How To Do It

> **What to Expect**
>
> The intervention itself, at last! It covers three theories and is easy to deliver along with details of who can deliver, and how. It is differentiated by key stage with the goals of the intervention, and there's a reminder not to deliver this intervention in isolation but as part of a whole School Development Plan tackling a test-taking culture in the school from the roots upwards.

> **Key Terms**
>
> **metacognition:** how students know what they know
> **priming anxiety:** talking about test anxiety too near to the exams themselves
> **recall aids recall:** every time you remember, it makes it easier to remember
> **Schemes of Work for 9-18-year-olds and beyond:** some say 'Programmes of Study'; it's the guidelines to the lessons you deliver
> **test anxiety; self-efficacy; the testing effect:** three theories combine to produce the intervention
> **testing effect:** or retrieval practice, testing and quizzing yourself

The Intervention is Easy to Deliver

The research for this intervention was situated in a real educational context in the messy setting of primary classrooms and subsequently in secondary schools (e.g. McKenney and Reeves, 2013). It is important that an intervention exists not for the sake of educational research but to address a real problem. This research included the design and testing of an intervention to address a problem in practice – the problem of **test anxiety**. It is a real-world intervention (e.g. McKenney and Reeves, 2013). It was important to me as I was researching that the intervention could be easily administered in any classroom by any adult (e.g. Brown, 1992). This is because, as a teacher for many years, I know the limits of being able to quickly adapt and adopt new practice. There are always so many demands on teachers, which is why this intervention has really been designed to be easily administered.

The design of the intervention in this study is the combination of three theories:

- the cognitive theory of **the testing effect** (e.g. Roediger and Karpicke, 2006b)
- test anxiety theory (e.g. Zeidner, 1998), and
- **self-efficacy theory** (Bandura, 1997).

It is the combination of these three theories that do real work (Cobb et al., 2003, p. 10).

The experiment is designed to address the problem of test anxiety that is both scientifically and practically important in school evaluative situations with the hope of improving student wellbeing around tests. This study demonstrates how the cognitive theory of the desirable difficulty, the testing effect (Bjork, 1975), can be used in primary and secondary classrooms to try to increase feelings of self-efficacy and potentially reduce test anxiety in students.

Nitty Gritty

We are getting to it now! Three versions are offered here to cater for the different ages, but the principles remain the same. The aim is to teach the students how memory works so they can revise effectively and then, because they have knowledge of/and used optimal revision techniques, they can reassure themselves about the knowledge that is in their long-term memory and readily available for the exam. They have been recalling, so they can recall under pressure. Their 'testing routes are well-oiled'.

The Intervention

The learning goals are to:

- learn how the testing effect works
- teach students **metacognition** of learning in order to gain self-efficacy in test taking
- teach students about the testing effect (Bjork, 1975) and how memory works – that **recall aids recall**, increases feelings of self-efficacy and reduces the cognitive or worry element of test anxiety.

To date, it has not been common practice to teach cognition of the testing effect to students to help students cope with evaluative situations.

A Reminder for Roots Deep Work

A golden thread of recommendation runs through this book: that the PSHE/Pastoral **Scheme of Work** cannot stand alone. A whole School Development Plan aimed at giving back control and reducing test anxiety is included in Chapter 9. The PSHE/Pastoral Scheme of Work here is the curriculum part of the School Development Plan, but a whole change in the way we think about tests is needed.

Soapbox: *Indeed, we need a whole change in the way we test in order to get the best from our youngsters – but that is for another day ...*

Year Groups and Delivery

This PSHE/Pastoral Scheme of Work (SoW) can be delivered to Years 5 and above all the way through to A level and indeed beyond. The PSHE/Pastoral Scheme of Work is divided into age groups, but you could mix and match according to your knowledge of your students. The Schemes of Work are as follows:

- SoW 1: Primary/KS2 (10–11-year-olds)
- SoW 2: Secondary/KS3 (11–14-year-olds)
- SoW 3: Secondary/KS4 (14–16-year-olds), and
- SoW 4: Secondary/KS5 and beyond (16–18-year-olds and upwards)

The lessons are designed to be delivered easily by a teacher, but that person will need some knowledge of desirable difficulties – hence the teacher training programme that is part of Chapter 8.

These units can be mixed and matched across key stages and ages but, in principle, at least each key stage should receive their unit once: e.g. for KS3 perhaps in Year 7 and repeat in Year 9. It is possible to 'do' something every year by accessing resources from the other year groups and creating a hybrid that suits your setting.

A Couple of Things to Note

Questionnaires

You will find copies of the questionnaires in the Appendices at the back of this book.

- Appendix A is the Children's Test Attitude Questionnaire
- Appendix B is the Children's Test Anxiety Questionnaire

It is important students complete both questionnaires and SoWs are delivered ahead of, and a few weeks away from, any major exams to avoid the issue of **priming anxiety**. For example, if Year 11 students have mock exams in December prior to the real exams in May, this unit could be delivered in the first half term of the academic year in September. You should aim to leave six weeks clear before high-stakes tests/exams *after* delivering this unit.

Documents

At the end of each Scheme of Work you will find versions of the documents that you can reproduce for your students. They are listed in this 'quickie' table below for ease of reference and checking.

Scheme of Work 1: Primary/KS2 (10-11-year-olds)

Appendix A: Children's Test Anxiety Scale Questionnaire
Appendix B: How Confident Are You? Questionnaire
Document 1 (SoW 1): Cognitive scientists in conversation
Document 2 (SoW 1): What the scientists said (questions for students on Document 1, SoW 1)
Document 3 (SoW 1): Facts about mushrooms
Document 4 (SoW 1): Questions about mushrooms
Document A: A letter from Bob

Scheme of Work 2: Secondary/KS3 (11-14-year-olds)

Appendix A: Children's Test Anxiety Scale Questionnaire
Appendix B: How Confident Are You? Questionnaire
Document 1 (SoW 2): Discussion on learning with cognitive scientists
Document 2 (SoW 2): Questions about what Roddy and Jeffrey think
Document 3 (SoW 2): Questions about what Bob thinks
Document A: A letter from Bob
Document B: Text from an exam-anxious friend

Scheme of Work 3: Secondary/KS4 (14-16-year-olds)

Appendix A: Children's Test Anxiety Scale Questionnaire
Appendix B: How Confident Are You? Questionnaire
Document 1 (SoW 3): How you learn
Document 2 (SoW 3): Learning biases
Document A: A letter from Bob
Document B: Text from an exam-anxious friend

Scheme of Work 4: Secondary/KS5 and beyond (16-18-year-olds and upwards)

Appendix A: Children's Test Anxiety Scale Questionnaire
Appendix B: How Confident Are You? Questionnaire
Document 1 (SoW 4): Judgements of learning
Document 2 (SoW 4): New Theory of Disuse
Document 3 (SoW 4): Strategies
Document A: A letter from Bob
Document B: Text from an exam-anxious friend

84 *Supporting Children and Young People with Test Anxiety in School*

You will see from this table that (in addition to the Questionnaires) two of the documents are used multiple times:

- Document A: A letter from Bob
- Document B: Text from an exam-anxious friend

These are included here, ahead of the Schemes of Work, so that you can reproduce and use them whenever they are referred to.

Document A (all SoWs): A letter from Bob

Bob, Roddy, Elizabeth, John, Carol and Jeffrey had a meeting this week and wondered if they had got any messages across to you. They are so desperate to give you good learning skills. Bob is quite worried, so he wrote you a letter:

'To those of you who are students, we hope we have convinced you to take a more active role in your learning by introducing **the testing effect** into your own study activities. Above all, try and rid yourself of the idea your memory works like a tape or video recorder and that re-reading the same material over and over again will somehow write it into your memory. Rather, assume that learning requires an active process of interpretation – that is, mapping new things we are trying to learn onto what we already know.

'Be aware, too, when re-reading a chapter or your notes, that prior exposure (having read them a few times before) creates a sense of familiarity that can easily be confused with understanding. And perhaps most importantly, keep in mind that retrieval (recalling the information), much more than restudying, acts to modify (to change) your memory by making the information that you practise retrieving more likely to be recallable again and in different contexts. In short, try to spend less time on the input side and more time on the output side, such as summarizing what you have read from memory, or getting together with friends and asking each other questions. Any activities that involve testing yourself – that is, activities that require you to retrieve or generate information, rather than just presenting information to yourself – will make your learning both more durable and flexible.

'Finally, we cannot overstate the importance of learning how to manage your own learning activities. In a world that is ever-more complex and rapidly changing, and in which learning on one's own is becoming ever-more important, *learning how to learn is the ultimate survival tool*.'

Reply to Bob Bjork (he generally hangs out at the University of California, Los Angeles) and advise him how you are going to 'learn how to learn so that you have the ultimate survival tool' for the future. You could probably say 'Dear Bob not Mr. Bjork'. You can use the back of this sheet to write or your notebook.

Document B (all SoWs): Text from an exam-anxious friend

A friend has texted you today. He is really worried about the exam tomorrow. He is worried he will fail and disappoint his parents, and also not get to study the A levels he wants, and he is generally just really stressing. He took an exam before and failed because, although he had worked really hard, he became so nervous, he couldn't remember anything. He remembers how upset he was then.

You know that he has been studying hard for the exam. He has been testing himself and answering test questions using short answers and looking up any mistakes. Also, he has been mixing up his revision and looking up answers when he has forgotten stuff. Two nights ago, all of you got together and tested each other. Your teacher regularly tests you in class and you have been following a PSHE/Pastoral unit about how testing works on memory. In other words, you **know** that every time you recall an answer it makes it easier to recall the information again. You **know** that this means that everything you revise goes into the long-term memory where it can be accessed even in exam conditions.

What advice will you give this friend? Write it down on the back of this sheet.

Scheme of Work 1: Primary/KS2 (10-11-year olds)

Week 1
- **Ask students to complete two questionnaires and hand back to you:** Appendix A: Children's Test Anxiety Scale, and Appendix B: How Confident Are You? Make sure you have the students' initials on the questionnaires. (You can then use the information in Chapter 1 to determine who are the most test-anxious students. However, this Scheme of Work is delivered to everyone.)
- In groups ask the students to brainstorm the words 'desirable difficulties'. Elect a group leader who will feed back the ideas from the brainstorm. Place as a display or photograph for PSHE/Pastoral evidence.

Week 2
- **Starter:** Ask: *Does anyone know what a cognitive scientist is and what they do?* You could then run a group chat and/or feedback.
- Tell the students they are going to act out a conversation between five cognitive scientists having a coffee. See *Document 1 (SoW 1): Cognitive scientists in conversation*.
- Students, in groups of five (or thereabouts), act out the café conversation. Ask each group to summarise the main points.

Week 3
- Ask students if they can remember the key points of the story from Week 2.
- Using *Document 2 (SoW 1): What the scientists said* (with questions for students on *Document 1, SoW 1*), explain the testing effect and the difference between 'study, study, study, test' (group 1); 'study, test, study, test, study, test' (group 2); and the most effective 'study, test, test, test' (group 3).
- Tell students that you are conducting an experiment and put them into three groups (as above), assigning one student to the teacher role for each group. Give each group a short fact sheet (see *Document 3 (SoW 1): Facts about mushrooms*) that they have to learn by using the three different methods above and apply the three different methods. You should also hand out *Document 4 (SoW 1): Questions about mushrooms*. (20 minutes)
- Then ask which groups they think learned the most and why.
- Give students the correct answer if they do not say the 'study, test, test, test' group and ask more able students to explain why. (*Recall aids recall even after a longer time. The other two groups may remember well for the test but it's likely they will have forgotten in a couple of weeks' time.*)

Week 4
- Ask students how they learn? Are they robots that can regurgitate information? Ask them how they revise. How do they know what they know?
- Change the groups around from Week 3 and repeat the experiment.
- Take general feedback about how the students felt about the change in technique?

Week 5
- Rotate the groups for a final time. This ensures everyone has experienced the different ways of studying.
- Take feedback on how students felt with the latest change.
- Ask groups to discuss and then summarise in a paragraph what they have learned about the testing effect so far.

Week 6
- In groups, ask students what the phrase 'Your testing routes are well-oiled' mean? Take feedback.
- Read the class a letter from the cognitive scientist Bob Bjork (*Document A: A letter from Bob*).
- Ask the students to reply in writing in their notebooks. Then read out some of their versions.

Week 7
- You could ask students to re-do the questionnaires (*Appendix A* and *Appendix B*) if you wish to get a measure of the effectiveness of the Scheme of Work.
Ask students the following questions and take answers:
  - What is the best way to revise? ('*study, test, test, test*')
  - Why?
  - What is the main problem with the 'study, study, study test' method? Or the 'study, test, study, test, study, test' method?
  - How does 'the testing effect' help with taking exams?
  - What can/should they text each other or say to each other before an important exam?
  - Do you have a 'positive test representative' in school? Should you? What would their job description look like?

Copyright material from Helen Barsham (2026) *Supporting Children and Young People With Test Anxiety*, Routledge

You could extend Scheme of Work 1 to an optional extra week in which you show a TED Talk by Carol Dweck titled 'The Power of Yet' (it's about 11 minutes long; you'll find the link in the Reference section). Ask students what they have learned about how the brain works from this.

You could also run an optional task: a job description for a 'Positive Test Person' role.

Scheme of Work 1: Primary/KS2 (10-11-year-olds)

Document 1: Cognitive scientists in conversation

Once upon a time, there lived five very famous cognitive scientists. And you know what a cognitive scientist does, don't you?

Bob, Elizabeth, Jeffrey, Roddy and Carol were all in a well-known café having their morning lattes. They were discussing their university students. All the cognitive scientists were teaching undergraduate courses in Psychology, and they had some worries about the amount of content that the students had to learn for their upcoming exams.

This was their conversation (they all have American accents).

Bob *I wish my students were robots. There is so much to learn for these new Psychology exams and computers/robots can just recall information; we humans can't. We humans need to link the learning and we need to keep remembering it for it to go into the long-term memory. Memory is not a machine; it likes cues and elaboration. Basically, every time you try and remember something, it makes it easier to remember next time.*

Elizabeth *Yes, you're right Bob – as always. But our students aren't robots or computers. We need to tell them the right way to study and then make sure that they use it.*

Roddy *Well, we know the right way, don't we? Jeffrey and I have done a lot of research in this, haven't we Jeffrey?*

Jeffrey *Yep! Sure have.*

Roddy *We tried three different ways of studying. One group learned by studying three times and then testing themselves; the second group studied 'study, test, study, test, study, test'; and the last group studied the text once but then tested themselves three times.*

Carol *Which group learned the best?*

Jeffrey *It was the last group – the ones who studied just once but tested themselves three times.*

Elizabeth *So let me get this right: one group did 'study, study, study, test' – Group 1. The second group did 'study, test, study, test, study, test' – Group 2. The third group did 'study, test, test, test' – Group 3.*

Roddy *Yep, that's right.*

Carol *So why is it the group that only studies once but tested the most learned the best?*

Bob and Elizabeth *We can answer that!*

Bob *It's like I was saying: we're not computers or robots and we learn by making mistakes, forgetting things and then remembering them, and because testing yourself is harder than re-reading something or repeated studying and the brain works harder, the memory likes it more and retains it. It keeps it safe for the long-term.*

Roddy *Yep that's right because the other two groups were fine for taking a test a day later or so, but when we tested them a week later, they had forgotten the facts whereas the group that tested the most retained the facts for longer.*

Carol *So it's ok to use 'study, study, study, test' or 'study, test, study, test, study, test' if you have a test the next day but not if you need to really remember stuff?*

Jeffrey Well I guess so but that's not the ideal way to study. It's leaving it all a bit late and can get stressful.

Bob You know, even if you know nothing about something – say, how the heart works – but you test yourself before you learn it, the information goes in better because you've kinda 'cued' it into the memory.

Carol This is all so fascinating and I'm wondering how this can help students.

Bob If we can get kids to study properly by testing themselves more than re-reading and highlighting stuff, they will have the knowledge properly in their brains. If knowledge is in the long-term memory, it's a big help to them in their exams.

Carol That's cool. That would mean it's definitely there for when they take exams.

Bob Yes. What's more, if they just keep telling themselves that they've revised properly – you know, that they have 'oiled their testing routes' (and they have done this) – they'll feel a lot better about taking exams.

Elizabeth It's great to think something as simple as just revising properly by testing can really help kids manage all these exams they have to take.

Carol So why don't they do that already?

Bob It's odd they behave like robots and think they can just recall knowledge without practising the testing. We have seen they must practise testing, but it takes more effort than just re-reading or 'blocking' as I call it – it's harder to try and remember.

Roddy Yes, but it's stronger and goes into the long-term memory so the kids are learning this stuff for life and not just for a test.

Bob I've told my students this, but they don't seem to believe me that blocking is really only useful if you're tested straight after and not useful if the exam is in a week's time.

Elizabeth We need to keep trying – we need to tell kids when they're younger so that they get the message sooner and so that they get into good, testing revision habits.

Jeffrey Yep, then if they feel nervous about exams they don't need to, because if they revise through testing, the knowledge is there and their access to the knowledge. 'Their testing routes have indeed been well oiled.'

All Right guys we're on a mission now! You know this is just about quizzing yourself on everything you learn; going home from a day at school and college and just trying to remember what you've learned that day.

Scheme of Work 1: Primary/KS2 (10-11-year-olds)

Document 2: What the scientists said

Bob, Jeffrey, Roddy, Carol and Elizabeth are very wise scientists and have said many wise words about how best to learn. We would be very daft if we don't take this advice. They say:

Good test performance following an all-night cramming or blocking session is certainly rewarding, but little of what was recallable on the test will remain recallable over time. In contrast, a study schedule that spaces study sessions on a particular topic and uses testing regularly can produce both good exam performance and good long-term retention.

What does this mean?

_____
_____
_____
_____
_____
_____
_____
_____
_____
_____

Roddy and Jeffrey ran a series of experiments in 2008. They found that *'study, test, test, test'* helps children learn more and perform better in tests than *'study, study, study, test'*. Summarise this in your own words.

_____
_____
_____
_____
_____
_____
_____
_____

Copyright material from Helen Barsham (2026) *Supporting Children and Young People With Test Anxiety*, Routledge

Scheme of Work 1: Primary/KS2 (10-11-year-olds)

Document 3: Facts about mushrooms (or make up your own useful factsheet)

Students should form three groups, which they rotate over the next three weeks. Each week, feedback from the groups should be shared about how they feel about their learning experiences.

Group 1: Read the fact sheet three times, and then test.
Group 2: Read the factsheet then test. Read again then test again. Read for a third time, then test again.
Group 3: Read the fact sheet once only, then test, then test, then test.

MUSHROOMS

Mushrooms are fascinating. They are very old and have been on Earth since about 1.2 billion to 1.5 billion years ago. The largest organism in the world is a fungus. Indeed, a honey fungus called *Armilllaria Ostoyae* was discovered in Oregon Forest and covered 2,384 acres.

When looking at a mushroom, you see the top of the fungus or the fruit. Most of the fungus lives underground in networks made up from small threads called *hyphae*.

Fungus plays an important role in ecology. *Saprotrophic* fungi use enzymes to break down substances and they can get rid of rotting leaves and logs. They can break down the tough compounds such as cellulose and pectin. In turn, this creates a healthy soil. On top of that, there are over 100 species of fungi that can destroy plastics.

Bioluminescent mushrooms (mushrooms that glow) are found across various continents, with species like *Mycena luxaeterna* found in the rainforests of São Paulo, Brazil, while others, such as *Omphalotus olearius*, are found across Europe and parts of South Africa.

The *Chaga* mushroom (*Inonotus obliquus*) is called the king of medical mushrooms. It is rich in antioxidants and can boost immunity, brain and liver health and possibly make you live longer.

Maitake mushrooms are used in Japan and China to treat diabetes and hypertension. They contain a complex sugar called beta-glucan. *Maitake* extract can stimulate the immune system.

YOU SHOULD NEVER EAT A MUSHROOM THAT YOU PICK (UNLESS YOU ARE AN EXPERT). SOME ARE TOXIC!

Scheme of Work 1: Primary/KS2 (10-11-year-olds)
Document 4: Questions about mushrooms

1. How long have mushrooms been on the Earth?

_____

Giving Back Control/Reducing Test Anxiety/How To Do It 93

2. How big was the honey fungus that was discovered in Oregon Forest?
___

3. What are the underground threads of a mushroom called?
___

4. Name the fungi that can break down rotting leaves and logs in this article.
___

5. What is the name of the bioluminescent fungus found in Brazil?
___

6. What is the name of the mushroom that is found across Europe and parts of South Africa?
___

7. What is the normal name for the king of medical mushrooms and a bonus point if you can give the Latin name too?
___

8. What are the health benefits of the mushroom in question 7?
___

9. Which mushroom is used in Japan and China to treat hypertension and diabetes?
___

10. What must you **NEVER** do with a mushroom that you pick?
___

(All questions carry 1 mark apart from Q7, which has 2 marks if you get the bonus question right. Make a note of your marks alongside your answers.)

Copyright material from Helen Barsham (2026) *Supporting Children and Young People With Test Anxiety*, Routledge

Scheme of Work 2: Secondary/KS3 (11-14-year-olds)

Week 1
- **Ask students to complete two questionnaires and hand back to you:** Appendix A: Children's Test Anxiety Scale, and Appendix B: How Confident Are You? Make sure you have the students' initials on the questionnaires. (You can then use the information in Chapter 1 to determine who are the most test-anxious students. However, this Scheme of Work is delivered to everyone.)
- With students in groups, explain that we are learning how to learn and ask them to brainstorm these terms:
  1. 'desirable difficulties'
  2. 'the testing effect'
  3. 'interleaving and spacing'
  4. 'cues and elaboration'
- Elect group leaders who will feed back the ideas from brainstorm.
- Take the feedback and place as a display or photograph for PSHE/Pastoral evidence.

Week 2
- **Recall:** What are 'desirable difficulties', 'the testing effect', 'interleaving and spacing' and 'cues and elaboration'?
- Ask students to read in groups *Document 1 (SoW 2): Discussion on learning with cognitive scientists* where they will learn about different approaches to learning.
- In groups, summarise the key points.

Week 3
- **Recall:** What were the cognitive scientists discussing?
- Complete *Document 2 (SoW 2): Questions about what Roddy and Jeffrey think*, and *Document 3 (SoW 2) Questions about what Bob thinks*. Take feedback.

Week 4
- **Recall:** Students read *Document A: A letter from Bob*, then reply to him.

Week 5
- **Time to try the experiment:** Which is better for a test after a week?

  Group 1: study, study, study, test
  Group 2: study, test, study, test, study, test, or
  Group 3: study, test, test, test

- Give the groups a topic they are all studying from the curriculum. Ask them to research it and devise a quiz using the material.
- They will have to compile the material - similar to *Document 3 (SoW 1): Facts about mushrooms* - and the questions. You can use *Document 3 (SoW 1)* if you get stuck, but it's better for students to create their own fact sheet that supports the curriculum. Indeed, this could be said for upper primary, too, so over to you on how you manage this.

Week 6 **Form student groups:**
Group 1: study, study, study, test
Group 2: study, test, study, test, study, test, or
Group 3: study, test, test, test

- Revise, using student fact sheets created in Week 5, then complete the test according to group instructions.
- Take feedback from each group as to how they do on the test?

Week 7
- Keep the same groups.
- Begin the lesson with the same test as Week 6 - the one the students created. Which groups did better this time?
- Give students *Document B: Text from an exam-anxious friend*. How would you respond to this text?

Copyright material from Helen Barsham (2026) *Supporting Children and Young People With Test Anxiety*, Routledge

Scheme of Work 2: Secondary/KS3 (11–14-year-olds)

Document 1: Discussion on learning with cognitive scientists

Professor Robert Bjork, Henry Roediger III (Roddy), Jeffrey Karpicke, Elizabeth Bjork, Carol Dweck and John Dunlosky are hanging out in a coffee shop discussing the best ways for the Psychology students to learn.

Roddy The best way is to test yourself – let a bit of forgetting set in then test yourself.

Jeff Yes. It's no good reading and re-reading, and then testing yourself because you will remember the stuff for that test but you won't be able to recall it a week later.

Bob You're talking about blocking or cramming for a test – it's like putting on a rucksack of knowledge then as soon as the test is finished, the knowledge is gone. We need to teach these kids how memory works. Memory likes cues and elaboration.

Roddy Yes. If you think about memory athletes – you know the guys who can remember decks of cards – they often use images or pictures to help them remember.

Elizabeth Anything you can do to make the learning memorable: do it standing on your hand, change the room you're in, sing it, make up funny sayings, use mnemonics, you need pegs to hang stuff on like the spelling of necessary ('one collar two shirt sleeves') – anything that will help memory remember.

Bob Goes back to what I was saying about these kids not being robots or computers – we're humans. Think how easy it is for us to remember bad experiences – it's because of all the experiences we felt with that. Sometimes the smallest cue can help us remember. Think how many times people say 'I'll never forget that'. It's because something meaningful has happened around that thing so they remember.

Carol Yep but kids can't make all their exam learning meaningful.

Roddy No ... that's why they need to use retrieval practice or the testing effect. Testing is 150% more effective than re-reading or highlighting stuff. Yes, it's harder, but the learning lasts longer.

Jeff So kids these days need to keep testing themselves – that's the answer and you know if they do that the knowledge will never leave them.

Bob Every time they try to remember something – to recall it – they make it easier to remember.

Carol This is so cool. This should make kids feel better taking tests 'cos you know they do know this stuff.

Bob Yep we tried an experiment like that. We kept saying to the kids 'you know you do know this stuff because you have been being tested by your teachers' and it did make them feel better about taking exams.

Jeff The key is to look up if you get something wrong – you know, get some feedback. You know, another thing even testing yourself and getting the answer wrong is better than no testing at all.

Roddy What's the best way for, like, 11–14-year-olds to learn for their exams?

John Hey guys … I've just been listening to y'all but honestly they do need to test – you know, practise retrieval practice – but they need to mix it up and leave some gaps so that they forget stuff. This makes it a lot of effort but it's the best way. For example, say you have some big exams coming up in six weeks' time in Maths, Geography and Biology. Don't read, then read, then read, or study, study, study, and then test because you'll get a good score on that test but it's fake – you know, because if you test yourself a week later you can't remember that stuff. You need to test a bit of Maths – look up anything you get wrong – then maybe learn the volcanoes in geography – same thing – and then photosynthesis in biology … and keep mixing up the revision and the learning. Also, while I'm on one – testing is so good for memory but the best tests are ones that need short answers, so not so much your multiple choice.

Elizabeth It all sounds so effortful – you know, having to remember – but I do remember getting something really wrong in a lecture I was giving and I never forgot that correction I made – they call it a hypercorrection – nothing like making a mistake to get it right!

Bob Yep, but we're trying to get this right for kids before they do make a big mistake – but I do agree with you – making a mistake – getting something wrong and then getting it right – really cues information into the brain. Memory likes this. I wish we didn't have to test kids; I wish there was another way.

Jeff Roddy you had a good idea?

Roddy Yep – until we come up with a better system: these kids should keep a testing diary … you know, a record of what they test themselves on and when and how they do. It would help us with our research if they did this.

Carol That's a genius idea and then they can monitor what they really know. I think we do really need to tell them though that if they do study, study, study, test – you know, just re-reading and then test – it's a fake outcome …

Elizabeth Yep. We said that once but it's important that these kids understand that that system is just learning for a test that's like immediate, not for when they have lots of tests in a row like the UK GCSEs for example.

Bob It's hard work, but simply summed up in 'study, test, test, test' is the best thing you can do – leave some time to let yourself forget, so that remembering is harder. It sounds daft but it works. And mix it up – that way you are spacing the learning out. Keep a record of how you're doing, and bad scores are good to start with. At the end of six weeks though those scores need to be going up, but it does mean you'll never forget that stuff about volcanoes – you'll be telling it to the grandkids! And yeah – even testing yourself or teachers testing kids on a subject they have never learned is really great for when they do come to learn it. The Brain remembers it better because it can tag the answer onto the question they didn't know the answer to in the first place.

Jeff This stuff can really help kids who hate taking those exams!

Giving Back Control/Reducing Test Anxiety/How To Do It

Scheme of Work 2: Secondary/KS3 (11-14-year-olds)

Document 2: Questions about what Roddy and Jeffrey think

You've read a long discussion between cognitive scientists about the best ways to learn. Now answer these questions.

Definitions

retention: what the memory can remember for a long time
    material: the topic being studied
    free recall: what can you remember without being prompted

---

1. Henry Roediger (Roddy to his friends) and Jeffrey Karpicke wrote many papers about cognition. What do you think the following title really means?:

'Test Enhanced Learning – Taking Memory Tests Improves Long-Term Retention'

_____
_____
_____
_____

2. Roddy and Jeffrey said: 'In two experiments, students studied prose (writing) passages and took one or three immediate free recall tests, without feedback, **or** they re-studied the prose material the same number of times as the students who received the tests. Students then took a final retention test at either 5 minutes, 2 days, or 1 week later. When the final test was given after 5 minutes, repeated studying improved recall compared to repeated testing. *However*, on the delayed tests, the earlier testing had produced greater retention than studying, even though repeated studying increased students' confidence in their ability to remember the material. Testing is a powerful means of improving learning, not just assessing it.'

What worked better? Studying or testing? Give reasons for your answer.

_____
_____
_____
_____
_____

Copyright material from Helen Barsham (2026) *Supporting Children and Young People With Test Anxiety*, Routledge

Do you like tests?

_____
_____

3. Roddy and Jeffrey also said: 'Practising the skills during learning that are needed for retrieval (testing) improves retention on memory tests. Although restudying the passages gives students all of the information again, testing allowed the students to practise the skill that they need for future tests and improved performance after a delay.

Can you summarise this in your own words?

_____
_____
_____
_____
_____

Is this something you would like to do?

_____
_____

4. Roddy and Jeffrey said: 'Students may prefer repeated studying because it produces short-term benefits, and students often learn ineffective learning strategies because they base their predictions of future performance on what produces rapid short gains. Although students in the repeated study conditions predicted they would perform very well a week later (compared to the other students who were just being tested), they actually performed the worst.'

What do you think to Roddy and Jeffrey saying this?

_____
_____
_____
_____
_____
_____

Copyright material from Helen Barsham (2026) *Supporting Children and Young People With Test Anxiety*, Routledge

Your final thoughts, please: What have you learned?

_____

_____

_____

_____

_____

_____

Scheme of Work 2: Secondary/KS3 (11-14-year-olds)

Document 3: Questions about what Bob thinks

> **Definitions**
> **interleaving**: mixing up subjects – let forgetting set in
>   **spacing:** rather than massing study sessions on a topic or 'blocking'
>   **using tests:** rather than studying again (Henry and Jeffrey approve)
>   **vary** the contexts: even **moving to a different room to study** can help.

Bob Bjork says we need *desirable difficulties* to learn well. These learning conditions can help you remember – even when you're old!

    Interleaving = mixing up two or more topics when you study, so study a bit of Math and then some Geography - just mixing up what you do – not doing one subject all at once.

    Spacing So imagine learning 20 French words then move onto your History revision. Hopefully you will forget some of the French words because letting the memory forget is a good thing. It means you need to make an effort to remember, and the information will stay in your memory for longer. Get it?

1. What is **interleaving**?

   _____
   _____
   _____
   _____
   _____
   _____

2. What is **spacing**?

   _____
   _____
   _____
   _____
   _____

3. Which is better and why? Testing yourself or re-reading?

_____
_____
_____
_____
_____
_____

4. Is moving to another room to study a good thing? Why?

_____
_____
_____
_____
_____
_____
_____

5. Bob is a very wise man and has said many wise words about how best to learn. We would be very daft if we don't take his advice below:

'Good test performance following an all-night cramming session is certainly rewarding, but little of what was recallable on the test will remain recallable over time. In contrast, a study schedule that spaces study sessions on a particular topic can produce both good exam performance and good long-term retention.'

What does Bob mean?

_____
_____
_____
_____
_____
_____

6. Thinking back to Roddy and Jeffrey, they ran a series of experiments in 2008. They found that 'study, test, test, test' helps children to learn more and perform better in tests than 'study, study, study, test'. Try to summarise this in your own.

_____
_____
_____
_____

7. How do you study? Are you happy with how you study? What might you change now that you have learned how to learn?

_____
_____
_____
_____
_____
_____
_____
_____
_____
_____
_____
_____
_____
_____
_____
_____
_____

Copyright material from Helen Barsham (2026) *Supporting Children and Young People With Test Anxiety*, Routledge

Scheme of Work 3: Secondary/KS4 (14-16-year-olds)

Week 1	• **Ask students to complete two questionnaires and hand back to you:** Appendix A: Children's Test Anxiety Scale, and Appendix B: How Confident Are You? Make sure you have the students' initials on the questionnaires. (You can then use the information in Chapter 1 to determine who are the most test-anxious students. However, this Scheme of Work is delivered to everyone.)
	• In groups, explain that we are learning how to learn and the most effective ways to revise, then ask the students to brainstorm these terms:
	1. 'desirable difficulties'
	2. 'the testing effect'
	3. 'interleaving and spacing'
	4. 'cues and elaboration'
	• Take feedback.
Week 2	• Ask students to read *Document 1 (SOW 3): How you learn* and take their feedback.
Week 3	• Give students *Document A: A letter from Bob* and *Document B: Text from an exam-anxious friend*.
	• Students should choose whether to write a response back to Bob Bjork or to their peer.
Week 4	• Watch the YouTube titled Learning to Learn: Conversation with Bob Bjork (Part 1: https://www.youtube.com/watch?v=fTtbp6TyBrI)
	• Ask groups to feedback key points.
	• Watch this YouTube a second time – do groups have any additional key points?
Week 5	• Ask: What are 'learning biases'?
	• Read *Document 2 (SoW 3): Learning biases*, then take feedback.
Week 6	• Talk the students through the experiment that KS3 students conducted by researching a topic they're studying and creating a fact sheet and test on this. (See Scheme of Work 2: Secondary/KS3 (11-14-year-olds).)
	• How would students in KS4 set up a memory experiment? What would they do? What would be the benefits to memory? Ultimately how would this help them with their GCSEs/exams? Listen to their thoughts, then ask them to set up their presentations.
Week 7	• Hear their memory presentations.

Copyright material from Helen Barsham (2026) *Supporting Children and Young People With Test Anxiety*, Routledge

Scheme of Work 3: Secondary/KS4 (14–16-year-olds)

Document 1: How you learn

One aspect of cognitive science is to study how people learn. You will be aware that over the next few years there is a lot of learning and a lot of testing. Listening to these famous cognitive scientists and what they say is the best way to learn so that you are prepared for multiple exams.

1. Bob Bjork said: 'Good test performance following an all-night cramming session is certainly rewarding, but little of what was recallable on the test will remain recallable over time. In contrast, a study schedule that spaces study sessions on a particular topic can produce both good exam performance and good long-term retention.'
2. Roddy and Jeffrey ran a series of experiments in 2008. They found that 'study, test, test, test' helps children learn more and perform better in tests than 'study, study, study, test'.
3. Roddy and Jeffrey said: 'In two experiments, students studied prose (writing) passages and took one or three **immediate** free recall tests, without feedback, **or** they re-studied the prose material the same number of times as the students who received the tests. Students then took a final retention test at either 5 minutes, 2 days, or 1 week later. When the final test was given after 5 min, repeated studying improved recall compared to repeated testing. However, on the delayed tests, the earlier testing had produced greater retention than studying, even though repeated studying increased students' confidence in their ability to remember the material. Testing is a powerful means of improving learning, not just assessing it.'
4. 'Students may prefer repeated studying because it produces short-term benefits, and students often learn ineffective learning strategies because they base their predictions of future performance on what produces rapid short gains. Although students in the repeated study conditions predicted they would perform very well a week later (compared to the other students who were just being tested) – they actually performed the worst.'
5. 'Practising the skills during learning that are needed for retrieval (testing) improves retention on memory tests. Although restudying the passages gives students all of the information again, testing allowed the students to practise the skill that they need for future tests and improved performance after a delay.'
6. John Dunlosky and his friends (see reference below) ran a series of experiments and found that testing is the best way to revise. Cramming or blocking for a test by re reading material only works if the test is the next day or imminent whereas practising interleaving and spacing of material – sometimes referred to as distributed practice help push material into the long-term memory. It is this method of revision that is needed to feel more confident when taking tests across multiple subjects and multiple weeks.

Read each statement. In groups discuss what this means and prepare to feedback to your teacher.

Extension task: Read Dunlosky et al., 2013.

Reference

Dunlosky, J., Rawson, K. A., Marsh, E. J., Nathan, M. J. & Willingham, D. T. (2013). Improving students' learning with effective learning techniques: Promising directions from cognitive and educational psychology. *Psychological Science in the Public Interest, 14*(1), 4-58.

Document 2: Learning biases

How well do you know yourself and how you learn? Read the following statements, discuss in your groups and then prepare to feed back what you think they mean in your own words.

1. *Hindsight* bias (Fischhoff, 1975) is an over-exaggeration of the likelihood of predicting an outcome before its occurrence. It is when we think we knew the information all along and this misconception can then affect what we study or learn for an exam. For example, you have just learned about the heart in Biology. You had a revision lesson in school followed by a test (*you will need to tell your teacher in the future that this is not the best way as they need to allow some forgetting to happen before testing!*). You do really well on the test, as does everyone who used their time well in the revision session. So, when it comes to revising for the main exam, you skip over the Heart stuff – well, you quickly read it through, but you don't re-test yourself because you did well in the class test. **Not a good idea!**
2. *Foresight* bias (Koriat and Bjork, 2006) is when easy recall of information, straight after reading a text, does not mean the information is learned but the learner thinks they will be able to reproduce this information again easily. It's quite a simplistic view really. You think you'll be able to do the same thing – easily recall the information in a week to two weeks' time! **Not a good idea!**
3. *Stability* bias (Kornell and Bjork, 2009) is where students believe their memories will not change in the future and assume that what they know now, they will always know and be able to recall. Memory does not work in this way.
4. Knowledge is not stored like a tape that can be played at will but needs constant elaboration, association, cue recall and relating to previous information (Bjork, 1975). We are not computers – well, not yet anyway! We need to recall information regularly for it to be easily recallable when we need it, for example in an exam. If you're interested in this stuff and how memory works, then ask your teacher for some information on the New Theory of Disuse (Bjork and Bjork, 1992).
5. DeWinstanley and Bjork (2004) discovered that when learners recognize the benefits that testing provides, they may adopt systems to help them engage in better encoding and better processing strategies for studying items to boost memory performance. Recognizing the benefits that testing provides could increase confidence, self-efficacy in test-taking, exam performance and ultimately, perhaps feelings of wellbeing.

Do you agree with the last sentence in statement 5? Explain your reasons.

Extension task: Why is forgetting good for you? Discuss or write your ideas.

References

Bjork, R. A. (1975). Retrieval as a memory modifier: An interpretation of negative recency and related phenomena. In R. L. Solso (ed.), *Information processing and cognition: The Loyola Symposium* (pp. 123-144). Mahway, NJ: Lawrence Erlbaum.

DeWinstanley, P. A. & Bjork, E. L. (2004). Processing strategies and the generation effect: Implications for making a better reader. *Memory & Cognition, 32*(6), 945-955.

Fischhoff, B. (1975). Hindsight is not equal to foresight: The effect of outcome knowledge on judgment under uncertainty. *Journal of Experimental Psychology: Human Perception and Performance, 1*(3), 288-299.

Koriat, A. & Bjork, R. A. (2006). Illusions of competence during study can be remedied by manipulations that enhance learners' sensitivity to retrieval conditions at test. *Memory & cognition, 34*(5), 959-972.

Kornell, N. & Bjork, R. A. (2009). A stability bias in human memory: Overestimating remembering and underestimating learning. *Journal of Experimental Psychology: General, 138*(4).

Scheme of Work 4: Secondary/KS5 and beyond (16–18-year-olds and upwards)

Week 1
- **Ask students to complete two questionnaires and hand back to you:** Appendix A: Children's Test Anxiety Scale, and Appendix B: How Confident Are You? Make sure you have the students' initials on the questionnaires. (You can then use the information in Chapter 1 to determine who are the most test-anxious students. However, this Scheme of Work is delivered to everyone.)
- Ask students to brainstorm these terms:
    1. 'desirable difficulties'
    2. 'the testing effect'
    3. 'interleaving and spacing'
    4. 'cues and elaboration'
- Take feedback.

Week 2
- Watch the YouTube titled Learning to Learn: Conversation with Bob Bjork (Part 1: https://www.youtube.com/watch?v=fTtbp6TyBrI)
- Read this paper (Dunlosky et al., 2013) and prepare to feedback on key points (see https://pubmed.ncbi.nlm.nih.gov/26173288/).

Week 3
- In group, design a PowerPoint presentation that teaches peers and lower year groups how they should revise and why?
- Invite groups to vote for the most informative and accurate presentation.

Week 4
- Suggest a presentation to a lower year group by the winning group. The rest of the year can complete further independent research into retrieval practice by using The Learning Scientists website (https://www.learningscientists.org).
- Alternatively, they could use the Effortful Educators website (https://theeffortfuleducator.com).
- A final option is the article 'Can teaching upper primary about the testing effect increase feelings of confidence about test-taking' (https://my.chartered.college/impact_article/can-teaching-upper-primary-about-the-testing-effect-increase-feelings-of-confidence-about-test-taking/)

Extension task: Students write their own blog/vlog for the school on the benefits of using retrieval practice or the testing effect to reduce test anxiety.

Week 5 **Metacognition of learning – problems with learning to learn.**
- Hand out *Document 1 (SoW 4): Judgements of learning*.
- Students answer this question: What are the problems with learning to learn? As part of their research, they should discuss with a teacher why students prefer blocking or cramming rather than interleaving study techniques and issues around testing.

Week 6
- Give students a copy of *Document 2 (SoW 4): New Theory of Disuse* to read. Then ask them to rewrite in their own words or draw what they read.

Students discuss why might writing about tests help anxiety about tests. Then they read Ramirez and Beilock, 2011, available at (https://www.science.org/doi/abs/10.1126/science.1199427). Give them *Document 3 (SoW 4): Strategies*.

- Finally, hand out *Document A: A letter from Bob* and *Document B: Text from an exam-anxious friend*. Think about, and write, your responses to either or both of these.

Optional extra: Students could write an argument for or against testing based on what they have learned. A further useful resource is Putwain, 2020: http://researchonline.ljmu.ac.uk/id/eprint/12214/

Scheme of Work 4: Secondary/KS5 and beyond (16-18-year-olds and upwards)

Document 1: Judgements of learning

Students really don't understand how they learn. This issue is discussed by Roediger and Karpicke (2006b) in an experiment about the meta-memory of prose passages. They found that students' judgements of learning (JoLs) felt that repeated study such as re-reading and highlighting were a better way to learn than repeated testing. In Bjork and Bjork (2019), the benefits of the desirable difficulty of interleaving over blocking or massed practice (cramming) are discussed. However, even when the results were shared, and the evidence was in front of them, the students in this experiment did not believe in these benefits. Bjork and Bjork (2019) discuss how to get students to believe in interleaving. In spite of being told that interleaving worked best and why it worked best, two thirds of the sample said they would still use a blocked method of teaching, if they were responsible for teaching that content.

The main problem is that learners believe and feel that blocking or cramming information in is better learning. Yan, Bjork and Bjork (2016) found that learners fail to appreciate **three main things:** the **benefits of testing** for learning, that **making mistakes** is good for learning, and **spacing rather than massing practice** or study leads to better long-term retention. Moreover, even though students were informed about the theory of interleaving as opposed to blocking, this knowledge did not alter their preference. Yan et al. (2016) were interested in why this belief exists and concluded that it is largely a result of years of conditioning. Learners have been taught to believe that blocking is better and because it feels easier, blocking must be better. Learners are also taught in blocks from an early age. Timetables are blocked. Classrooms themselves are in blocks. Subjects in a curriculum textbook are in blocks. But you know what – we're blocking the obtaining of real knowledge here. We are not encouraging free-range thinking or roaming of thought. To solve problems you need a little bit of information from here and there and then you pull all the strands together in a unique and brilliant solution – creative problem solving. We teach you to study a chapter in a textbook and then test you on it! Blocking! You could have an interesting discussion with your teachers as to why this might be? A lot of it is to do with how much content your poor teachers have to get through for exams!

In many cases, there may be students, who simply don't know how to learn McNamara (2010) suggests this problem is a result of educational systems that are focused on delivering content but not how the content can be learned. This view is endorsed by Hattie and Yates (2014, p. 162), who call it a paradox that teachers expect students to remember accurately and note that there is little instruction about how to remember.

Interestingly, when working with a younger age group, Lipowski et al. (2014) suggest 9- to 10-year-olds were able to understand the benefits of the testing effect. It is possible that a younger age group are able to understand aspects of cognitive theory such as the testing effect more readily than older students because they have used retrieval practice recently in classrooms and/or because they are not yet set in study habits such as blocked or massed practice.

References

Bjork, R. A. & Bjork, E. L. (2019). The myth that blocking one's study or practice by topic or skill enhances learning. In C. Barton (ed.), *Education myths: An evidence-informed guide for teachers*. Woodbridge: John Catt Educational Ltd.

Hattie, J., Yates, G. (2014). *Visible learning and the science of how we learn*. London and New York: Routledge.

Lipowski, S. L., Pyc, M. A., Dunlosky, J. & Rawson, K. A. (2014). Establishing and explaining the testing effect in free recall for young children. *Developmental Psychology, 50*(4), 994–1000.

McNamara D. S. (2010). Strategies to read and learn: Overcoming learning by consumption. *Medical Education, 44*(4), 340–346.

Roediger, H. L. & Karpicke J. D. (2006). Test-enhanced learning: Taking memory tests improves long-term retention. *Psychological Science, 17*(3), 249–255.

Yan, V. X., Bjork, E. L. & Bjork, R. A. (2016). On the difficulty of mending metacognitive illusions: A priori theories, fluency effects, and misattributions of the interleaving benefit. *Journal of Experimental Psychology, 145*(7), 918–933.

Scheme of Work 4: Secondary/KS5 and beyond (16-18-year-olds and upwards)

Document 2: New Theory of Disuse

Read through this document. Once you have done so, you should either try to express the ideas in your own words or, if you prefer a visual, try to draw what is happening in the brain with memory – how memory works.

In their book *New Theory of Disuse*, Bjork and Bjork (1992) explain two strengths of memory: **storage** and **retrieval** strength. If retrieval strength *increases*, then storage strength *decreases*. If retrieval strength is *high*, then storage strength is *low*. If there *is low* retrieval strength, then storage strength is *high*. In other words, the more difficult something is to recall, the longer it will stay in memory, as long as it can be remembered in the first place. However, if something is easy to remember, it may be forgotten quickly. This is the situation when you block or cram for a test. If you input all the knowledge just before an exam you can retrieve it – retrieval strength is high but storage low, so you won't remember this if the test is a week later! If you need to rely on your knowledge for your profession for example a doctor, you need to have strong storage strength.

Storage strength is how well item is learned and the degree of its strength is shown through the ease of its retrieval. To grow an item in storage strength, you need to study and recall of items. There is no limit on storage strength but there is a limit on retrieval strength. If retrieval strength is strong it is assumed to slow down storage strength's ability to store the knowledge. This is because retrieval strength is cue dependent and as certain items increase in retrieval strength, others are less recallable, but they are in the storage of the brain but they just get pushed to the back a bit.

Think of storage strength as a very large attic where knowledge is stored, and which can never be filled up. There is always plenty of space. However, if you don't take an item out regularly to use, it becomes dusty and stuck at the back and can be difficult to find when you need it, but it is still there. The piles of knowledge at the entrance to the attic, which you use often (when you retrieve them regularly through testing) aren't dusty and can be found quickly and are easily accessible, these are retrieval strength. Sometimes, if you're using a lot of recalled ideas from one recent pile, you may forget to take some of the items from another recent pile (retrieval induced forgetting). Ideally, you need to be able to reach the dusty old knowledge at the back and the way to do this is to keep moving the items in the attic around (interleaving, spacing and retrieval practice can do this) so that they all have a turn at being accessible and all have a turn at being at the back. This way you are increasing your storage strength while maintaining your retrieval strength, which is the ideal to have both of these working strongly for you. The way to do this is to constantly interleave the retrieval so that nothing, no knowledge gets dusty. Successful retrieval has a larger impact on both storage strength and retrieval strength than re-study: this is the testing effect.

Memory has a semantic relationship to items' schemas and scripts already in the long-term memory. When memory encounters strong new information, there is plenty of storage 'in the attic'; remember there is unlimited storage space. It is also a magical attic where

the space just keeps on increasing. The more knowledge we have, the more ways to store additional knowledge.

As humans, we are impressive at getting information into the brain (up into the attic), but not so good at getting it out (once it's got lost and dusty at the back). Memory is a modifier (Bjork, 1975) because once we can recall where we stored the information (in the attic), we can find the same path again quickly. The information retrieved becomes more retrievable. 'The testing routes are well-oiled.' (Your attic map is working!) However, other information becomes less retrievable (a neglected pile in the attic or a lost route on the map). Some items become non recallable with disuse. These are the ones you cannot find in your attic at all, but they are still there.

To make the most of memory skills, you should practise a **delayed initial recall** of the material and **delay re-study**. The key is to make the initial learning process **difficult or effortful**; allow some forgetting to have happened before retrieval is attempted. This method decreases retrieval strength and makes performance worse but enhances learning and later recall (e.g., Pyc and Rawson, 2010). So, if you are learning for a test or exam, don't cram or block by study, study, study then test, but study then test, test, test but **delay the first test** so that you have forgotten some of the material because then when you can't remember or have to look it up memory will just love this and will start to give it storage strength.

References

Bjork, R. A. (1975). Retrieval as a memory modifier: An interpretation of negative recency and related phenomena. In R. L. Solso (ed.), *Information processing and cognition: The Loyola Symposium* (pp. 123-144). Mahway, NJ: Lawrence Erlbaum.

Bjork, R. A. & Bjork, E. L. (1992). *A new theory of disuse and an old theory of stimulus fluctuation*. In A. F. Healy, S. M. Kosslyn & R. M. Shiffrin (eds.), *Essays in honor of William K. Estes, Vol. 1. From learning theory to connectionist theory; Vol. 2. From learning processes to cognitive processes* (pp. 35-67). Mahway, NJ: Lawrence Erlbaum Associates, Inc.

Pyc, M. A. & Rawson, K. A. (2010). Why testing improves memory: Mediator effectiveness hypothesis. *Science, 330*(6002), 335.

Scheme of Work 4: Secondary/KS5 and beyond (16-18-year-olds and upwards)

Document 3: Strategies

Do you think that writing down positive or negative thoughts can help with anxiety? Journalling is often recommended as a well-being strategy. There is some research to suggest that writing down positive affirmations and/or ridding yourself of negative thoughts before an exam may help those of you who have anxiety about taking exams.

You are asked as part of this unit to either

1. write a letter to Bob Bjork (Professor!) at his cognitive science laboratory in California (UCLA) and to address his concerns, or
2. address you friend's concerns.

You can do both if you wish. It would be really beneficial for you to consider what the advantages are of writing down thoughts and feelings prior to exams as you complete these tasks.

If you find any of the resources difficult or that you don't like, feel free to adapt for your own setting. These are pro formas for your tweaking.

Happy to help if you need it.

Email: helen@fighttestanxiety.com Web: fighttestanxiety.com

References and Further Reading

Bandura, A. (1997). *Self-efficacy: The exercise of control.* Stanford University, CA: W. H. Freeman/Times Books/Henry Holt & Co.
Barsham, H. & Ellefson, M. R. (2020) Can teaching upper primary about the testing effect increase feelings of confidence about test taking? *Journal of the Chartered College of Teachers, Impact 8.* /
Bjork, R. A. (1975). Retrieval as a memory modifier: An interpretation of negative recency and related phenomena. In R. L. Solso (ed.), *Information processing and cognition: The Loyola Symposium* (pp. 123-144). Mahway, NJ: Lawrence Erlbaum. https://bjorklab.psych.ucla.edu/wp-content/uploads/sites/13/2016/07/RBjork_1975.pdf
Bjork, R. A. (2014, March 30) Learning to learn. Conversation with Bob Bjork (Part 1) YouTube [video] https://www.youtube.com/watch?v=fTtbp6TyBrI
Bjork, R. A. & Bjork, E. L. (1992). *A new theory of disuse and an old theory of stimulus fluctuation.* In A. F. Healy, S. M. Kosslyn & R. M. Shiffrin (eds.), *Essays in honor of William K. Estes, Vol. 1. From learning theory to connectionist theory; Vol. 2. From learning processes to cognitive processes* (pp. 35-67). Mahway, NJ: Lawrence Erlbaum Associates, Inc. https://bjorklab.psych.ucla.edu/wp-content/uploads/sites/13/2016/07/RBjork_EBjork_1992.pdf
Bjork, R. A. & Bjork, E. L. (2019). The myth that blocking one's study or practice by topic or skill enhances learning. In C. Barton (ed.), *Education myths: An evidence-informed guide for teachers.* Woodbridge: John Catt Educational Ltd. https://bjorklab.psych.ucla.edu/wp-content/uploads/sites/13/2020/01/BjorkBjorkEducatinMythChapterPublishedFormSept2019.pdf
Brown, A. (1992). Design experiments: Theoretical and methodological challenges in creating complex interventions in classroom settings., *Journal of the Learning Sciences, 2*(2), 141-178. https://doi.org/10.1207/s15327809jls0202_2
Cobb, P., Confrey, J., DiSessa, A., Lehrer, R. & Schauble, L. (2003). Design experiments in educational research. *Educational Researcher, 32*(1), 9-13. https://doi.org/10.3102%2F0013189X032001009
DeWinstanley, P. A. & Bjork, E. L. (2004). Processing strategies and the generation effect: Implications for making a better reader. *Memory & Cognition, 32*(6), 945-955. https://doi.org/10.3758/bf03196872

Dunlosky, J., Rawson, K. A., Marsh, E. J., Nathan, M. J. & Willingham, D. T. (2013). Improving students' learning with effective learning techniques: Promising directions from cognitive and educational psychology. *Psychological Science in the Public Interest*, 14(1), 4-58. doi: 10.1177/1529100612453266

Dweck, C. The power of yet. YouTube, https://www.youtube.com/watch?v=J-swZaKN2Ic

Fischhoff, B. (1975). Hindsight is not equal to foresight: The effect of outcome knowledge on judgment under uncertainty. *Journal of Experimental Psychology: Human Perception and Performance*, 1(3), 288-299. https://doi.org/10.1037/0096-1523.1.3.288.

Harvard, B. (n.d.) The effortful educator. https://theeffortfuleducator.com

Hattie, J., Yates, G. (2014). *Visible learning and the science of how we learn*. London and New York: Routledge.

Koriat, A. & Bjork, R. A. (2006). Illusions of competence during study can be remedied by manipulations that enhance learners' sensitivity to retrieval conditions at test. *Memory & cognition*, 34(5), 959-972. https://doi.org/10.3758/bf03193244

Kornell, N. & Bjork, R. A. (2009). A stability bias in human memory: Overestimating remembering and underestimating learning. *Journal of Experimental Psychology: General*, 138(4). https://doi.org/10.1037/a0017350 https://www.learningscientists.org

Lipowski, S. L., Pyc, M. A., Dunlosky, J. & Rawson, K. A. (2014). Establishing and explaining the testing effect in free recall for young children. *Developmental Psychology*, 50(4), 994-1000. https://doi.org/10.1037/a0035202

McKenney, S. & Reeves, T. C. (2013). Systematic review of design-based research progress: Is a little knowledge a dangerous thing? *Educational Researcher*, 42(2), 97-100. https://doi.org/10.3102/0013189X12463781

McNamara D. S. (2010). Strategies to read and learn: Overcoming learning by consumption. *Medical Education*, 44(4), 340-346. /

Pyc, M. A. & Rawson, K. A. (2010). Why testing improves memory: Mediator effectiveness hypothesis. *Science*, 330(6002), 335. https://doi.org/10.1126/science.1191465

Putwain, D. W. (2020) *Examination pressures on children and young people: Are they taken seriously enough? A provocation paper*. The British Academy. https://medium.com/reframing-childhood-past-and-present/examination-pressures-on-children-and-young-people-are-they-taken-seriously-enough-e274b9595d4

Ramirez, G. & Beilock, S. L. (2011). Writing about testing worries boosts exam performance in the classroom. *Science (New York, N.Y.)*, 331(6014), 211-213. https://doi.org/10.1126/science.1199427

Roediger, H. L. & Karpicke J. D. (2006). Test-enhanced learning: Taking memory tests improves long-term retention. *Psychological Science*, 17(3), 249-255. https://doi.org/10.1111%2Fj.1467-9280.2006.01693.x

Yan, V. X., Bjork, E. L. & Bjork, R. A. (2016). On the difficulty of mending metacognitive illusions: A priori theories, fluency effects, and misattributions of the interleaving benefit. *Journal of Experimental Psychology*, 145(7), 918-933. https://doi.org/10.1037/xge0000177

Zeidner, M. (1998) *Test anxiety: The state of the art*. New York: Springer Science+Business.

7 Learning and Metacognition

> **What to Expect**
>
> This chapter looks at Judgements of Learning (JoLs) and why they are often incorrect. There are some soapbox moments as we discuss learning for life as opposed to learning for exams. There's the perils of blocking again, the joy of making mistakes and the lament of no time for these hugely beneficial learning techniques in the curricula. Young students understand the testing effect; they have not been indoctrinated with 'blocking'. The chapter also covers retrieval fluency (see blocking and biases and how can we monitor learning) and metacognition (how do we know what we know, really know, and not just kidding ourselves).

> **Key Terms**
>
> **biases:** how students know what they know, and when are they kidding themselves (see also Metacognition of Learning and Knowledge Biases from Chapter 3)
>
> **blocking:** this is a problem; students think it's effective, but it's only partially effective (if test is the next day) and certainly not helpful to test-anxious students
>
> **incorrect JoLs:** problem is, students think if they do well on a test, they know the material and don't bother revising it; they may know it for that test but not a later test (this is the problem of **retrieval fluency**)
>
> **judgements of learning (JoLs):** how you assess (judge) what you think you know
>
> **making mistakes:** one of the best things we can do if we want to remember something – full of cues and elaboration
>
> **monitoring metacognition:** how can we do this effectively? Ask students what they think. For sure, teach them about desirable difficulties, deliver the intervention and educate them about learning biases
>
> **spacing:** mixing revision schedules (teaching?) up, let forgetting set in, move on before mastery, recall incorrectly because spacing makes recall harder and when it's harder, it's stronger and lasts longer ... look it up, learn for life
>
> **younger students:** they aren't indoctrinated with 'blocked practice' – hopefully apart from spelling tests

Incorrect Judgements of Learning (JoLs) are a common problem that affect the long-term retention of learning. Many students are not able to judge their own learning (Bjork et al., 2013). In other words, *they don't know what they do and don't know.* Bjork et al. (2013) suggest that learners' metacognition is unsuccessful in understanding that successful retrieval is the key to retaining knowledge in the long-term memory. Sadly, the perception of being tested in schools and colleges is that testing is a means of assessing knowledge rather than learning (e.g. Bjork et al., 2013; Yang, Luo et al., 2021). Importantly, it is often dreaded or hated by students, as the contextual benefits of testing – *that of being recall that will aid future recall* – have often not been explained to the students.

The Reason For A Whole-School Development Plan

Here I return to an earlier point and the reason why a whole School Development Plan is included in this book. Although the Schemes of Works in Chapter 6 will help students to understand: (1) how memory works; (2) how they need to revise; (3) how they then actually feel more confident because they have been testing; and (4) as long as they interleave, space and don't cram, the knowledge will be in the long-term memory and accessible, this Scheme of Work will be far more effective if delivered against the whole-school context of a change in the way that tests are approached in the school.

In a Chapter 8 soapbox, I dream about being free to learn to learn and not to jump through blocked hoops of information that, in my opinion, are limiting the capacity for creative thinking. But while we still have the current system in place, we must find ways to navigate it, and changing a school's approach to testing along with the delivery of the PSHE/Pastoral Scheme of Work is a step in the right direction.

The Problem of Not Knowing What You Know

Back to the problem of knowing (or not knowing) what we know. The lack of realistic understanding students have about their own learning is discussed by Roediger and Karpicke (2006b) in an experiment about the meta-memory of prose passages. They found students' JOLs felt that repeated study (study, study, study, test) is better learning than repeated testing (study, test, test, test). Karpicke and Roediger (2008) report that students have no awareness of the effects of learning in memory. Bjork and Bjork (2019) discuss the benefits of interleaving study over **blocking** or massed practice for perceptual motor skills (such as learning different baseball strokes), verbal-conceptual procedural skills (learning algebra), and the long-term retention of knowledge and transfer skills. The benefits of interleaving were evident in all types of learning. However, and interestingly, the students in the experiment did not believe in these benefits.

Bjork and Bjork (2019) discuss how to get students to believe in interleaving. In spite of being told that interleaving worked best and why it worked best, two-thirds of the sample said they would still use a blocked method of teaching if they were responsible for teaching that content.

The problem runs deep and is probably a result of years of 'blocked' conditioning. The problem of misjudging what is known, for older students, is that they believe and feel blocking is better learning. Yan, Bjork and Bjork (2016) found that learners fail to appreciate three main things:

- the benefits of testing for learning
- that **making mistakes** is good for learning
- **spacing**, rather than massing practice or study, leads to better long-term retention. *Learners prefer non-optimal conditions for learning.*

Yan et al. (2016) investigated this problem further. They used a similar experiment to Kornell and Bjork (2008), which concluded that interleaving benefits are robust and effect size is large for benefiting inductive learning. The learners in Kornell and Bjork (2008) also reported that blocking, not interleaving, helped them to learn better.

Yan et al. (2016), in a similar way to Bjork and Bjork (2019), attempted to fix the illusion that blocking is more effective for learning, and this task was difficult. Although participants were informed about the theory of interleaving as opposed to blocking, this knowledge did not alter their preference. Yan et al. (2016) were interested in why this immoveable belief exists and concluded that it is largely a result of conditioning. Learners have been taught to believe that blocking is better and, because it feels easier, blocking must be better.

> **Nitty Gritty**
>
> Even when the research is in front of the students and they are presented with the facts of the learning situation, their conditioning over the years of being taught information for a test and then being tested on this information (massed or blocked learning) and being able to regurgitate it in those testing conditions, has become a reassuring habit. It feels secure, whereas interleaving and getting things wrong/making mistakes is unacceptable. The power of peer comparison and the way feedback is managed in schools is integral in this heady mix of:
>
> - being conditioned in blocked learning and testing
> - peer evaluation
> - perfection as portrayed on social media channels, and
> - the power of a highlighter pen.

Soapbox: *Somehow schools need to create a culture that can genuinely promote learning to learn for knowledge rather than performance. I think that is the purpose of education? When did education become a series of hoops to jump through cramming enough knowledge to get to the next stage?*

In many cases, there may be students, who simply don't know how to learn in an optimal way – although I expect that number is happily reducing given the prevalence of retrieval practice in classrooms (Bates and Shea 2024). McNamara (2010) suggests this problem is a result of educational systems that are focused on delivering content but not how the content can be learned. This view is endorsed by Hattie and Yates (2014, p. 162), who call it a paradox that teachers expect students to remember accurately and note that there is little instruction about how to remember. However, it may be that the educational climate is changing with the introduction of using retrieval practice or the testing effect into the Teacher Training Standards effective from 2020, and that Bates and Shea (2024) report that retrieval practice is happening in classrooms suggests teachers do it without even knowing they're doing it.

Retrieval Fluency

Another hindrance to judging learning effectively is discussed by Bjork et al. (2013) in the idea of **retrieval fluency.** This term means that the students believe they know the content because it is easily recallable. For example, reading a passage and then being tested on the material, immediately afterwards will produce easy and non-effortful retrieval that will make the student believe they know the material. Effortful retrieval is necessary and comes from delaying the initial recall of knowledge (e.g. Roediger and Karpicke, 2011).

> **In A Nutshell**
>
> Study, test, test, test, but delay the first test so that forgetting has set in. Remember that the memory likes cues, and getting something wrong or not being able to remember is a very fine thing to happen because it increases the storage strength of the information in the memory.

Soapbox: As a headteacher and senior leader in UK schools, I witnessed first-hand how colleagues struggled and continue to struggle to cover the content of the GCSEs (General Certificates in Education) that were introduced in 2017. Indeed, many schools now start GCSEs in Year 9 (13-14-year-olds) so they can cover the content over three years instead of two. As a headteacher, teacher (and mum), it concerns me that real learning techniques and a love of learning for life are being sacrificed because of the amount of content that has to be covered for a high stakes' test, which for many students becomes ten lots of blocked practice: a means to an end. Students need to get the grades to determine their sixth-form studies (16-18-years-old). Most of the knowledge is not revisited afterwards unless further exams are taken in that subject. It is the GCSE results that determine the A level (Advanced General Certificate in Education) options or further education courses at 15-16-years-old.

As an educator of 27 years, I know that in many educational contexts in both primary (particularly upper primary as preparation for secondary education) and secondary phases of education, the subjects studied are blocked. Many educational resources such as textbooks, are compiled in a blocked way, as are many examination syllabi. These exam syllabi and subsequent necessary timetabling blocks ('blocks' are what the subject groupings in timetables are sometimes called in the UK) may contribute to blocked or massed learning techniques.

Possible Solutions for Improving Students' Metacognition

These are the problems with assessing one's own learning but let's look to solutions. According to Kornell and Bjork (2009), there are two aspects to successful metacognition:

1. individuals need to know how memory works, and
2. individuals need to have the ability to monitor one's own memory.

This is what schools need to do. The Schemes of Work in Chapter 6 covering the different key stages address the first part of this problem.

Koriat and Bjork (2006) found two procedures that helped to mend metacognitive thinking:

1. teaching learners about **biases** in learning, and
2. making learners aware of mnemonic cues around the ease of retrieval.

These procedures provide people with valid knowledge of the cognitive system and encourage them to apply that knowledge in forming metacognitive learning strategies.

Nitty Gritty

A test-anxious student might become less test anxious if they are accurately and well informed about their learning journey. This metacognitive knowledge could alleviate test anxiety. This is why it is imperative that students are taught about how testing works on memory so that, while we still have the current system of exams, they can feel confident they have prepared the content/knowledge into their long-term memory through practising retrieval practice. This contextualizing of why a student needs to test might be all it takes to allow them to feel more confident about taking exams. 'Your testing routes are well-oiled. Recall aids recall.' Knowing about how learning works and using this knowledge as a coping strategy to manage test anxiety is the premise of the intervention in this study.

Monitoring Metacognition

The ability to monitor learning accurately and to notice differences in the acquisition of learning, and in testing and later testing, is not an easy process – especially given the sheer amount of content teachers and students have to get through. Monitoring of learning needs to be tracked, analysed and acted on by students and teachers. Students need support in this process, which is arguably more important than many other educational processes (e.g. Bjork et al., 2013; Hattie and Yates, 2014). Bjork et al. (2013) refer to the issue of students rarely being tested on *how* they learn to learn. *The problem is time*. With such heavy content blocked units of hoops of knowledge to jump through and over, who has time to consider what we actually know and how we know it?

As an experienced educator, I would suggest that, historically, students have not been taught how to learn or have been taught incorrectly. The Schemes of Work in Chapter 6 do test students on how they learn for tests through teaching them about memory and writing or presenting their new knowledge. This is teaching them that tests are learning events in themselves. Use the Schemes of Work in Chapter 6 and you've nailed the problem of teaching and testing students on how they learn.

> ### In A Nutshell
>
> For a student, **who is anxious about tests**, having a record of their learning during the learning process could feel very supportive and this self-knowledge could potentially be very empowering.

Learning to Learn is a Critical, Life Survival Skill

Bjork and Bjork (2011) suggest that knowing how to learn is a critical survival tool. Bjork et al. (2013) regard metacognition as the ultimate survival tool. One problem is that unless the test has been taken after some forgetting has happened, the perception of knowledge may be subject to retrieval fluency (Bjork et al., 2013).

Agarwal et al. (2008), in their study about the testing effect with open and closed book testing, suggest that students failed to predict the effectiveness of testing relative to studying. However, Agarwal et al. (2014) suggest that 92% of middle and high school students felt that retrieval practice helped their learning and 72% said that retrieval practice made them less anxious about tests. Perhaps this difference over time is a reflection of the way that classroom cultures are changing.

> ### Nitty Gritty
>
> Knowing that the testing effect is a cognitive process that promotes effective learning and retention of knowledge has important implications for educational practice.

Learning about learning is a skill in itself that can be taught (Pan and Bjork, 2021). It is this idea at the heart of this book's Schemes of Work because students are taught about how the testing effect works to give them the knowledge that their 'testing routes had been well-oiled' prior to high-stakes tests. As an educator over these 27 years, I think students should be taught the following key aspects about how to manage their learning:

- how memory works, and specifically the activities that help to store knowledge in the memory – in other words, retrieval practice and that retrieving information from memory is a memory modifier (Bjork, 1975)
- the role encoding plays in retrieval practice (Bjork et al., 2013), and
- the learning biases of *hindsight*, *foresight* and *stability* bias.

All of these aspects of metacognition of learning are covered in the PSHE/Pastoral Scheme of Work across the key stages. Mix and match as you need!

Biases

Hindsight bias (Fischoff, 1975) is when we think we knew the information all along, and this misconception can then affect what we study or learn for an exam.

Foresight bias (Koriat and Bjork, 2006) is when easy recall of information straight after reading a text does not mean the information is learned but the learner thinks they will be able to reproduce this information again easily.

Stability bias (Kornell and Bjork, 2009) is where students believe their memories will not change in the future and assume that what they know now, they will always know and be able to recall. Memory does not work in this way.

Soapbox: It is my opinion, as a teacher and educator, that the knowledge of these key aspects about how memory works and biases could transform what is learned in schools and the way it is learned.

In A Nutshell

Knowledge is not stored like a tape that can be played at will, but needs constant elaboration, association, cue recall and relating to previous information (Bjork, 1975).

DeWhinstanley and Bjork (2004) discovered that when learners recognize the benefits that testing provides, they may naturally engage in better encoding and processing strategies for studying items, during subsequent lists, to boost memory performance. Recognizing the benefits that testing provides could increase confidence, self-efficacy in test-taking, exam performance and, ultimately, perhaps feelings of wellbeing. I have measured self-efficacy in test-taking and worry in this study but not performance or wellbeing.

To address these misconceptions about learning, it is important to teach students to monitor their learning accurately. An accurate appraisal of the learning process might give mastery of one's own learning and a key tenet of self-efficacy is mastery (Bandura, 1997). This strategy could be a key for a student who has high levels of test anxiety. Learning about the testing effect may lead to self-efficacy in test-taking and a reduction in the worry or cognitive element of test anxiety.

Solving the Problem; Start Them Young

It would appear that the key to unlocking the blocks of metacognition is to teach students how memory works when they are younger. Lipowski et al. (2013) suggest that third grade students (9-10-year-olds) were able to understand the benefits of the testing effect. In my own experience as a researcher and teacher, I would confirm that the upper primary or elementary age group understand the testing effect. It is possible that younger student age-groups are able to understand aspects of cognitive theory such as the testing effect more readily than older students because they have used retrieval practice recently in classroom and/or because they are not yet set in study habits such as blocked or massed practice. Perhaps they are simply more open to ideas?

How Can Students Monitor Their Own Learning?

A possible suggestion is to keep a testing diary or a 'mistakes I made' diary or a 'what didn't I know', or some such document that covers all of these ideas. Whatever is decided, it cannot be onerous or take a lot of time. It could be an app on a phone? This would be a great problem for students to solve. They will know how they can do it! Perhaps there is no need to record the learning, as it becomes an administrative task serving no real purpose? I think we should ask them!

> ### Nitty Gritty
>
> The key is really in teaching all students, regardless of age, about the desirable difficulties, so they understand how the testing effect works and, ultimately, how memory works – that they know if they test themselves straight after studying something and get good marks they are probably not going to be able to do the same in a week's time because this is simply retrieval fluency. Older students can understand the New Theory of Disuse or the memory attic analogy. Just understanding how learning happens in the brain will aid their metacognition of what they know. It would also be helpful to ask them if they have an idea for how they can monitor their own learning better as part of the PSHE/Pastoral Scheme of Work or the whole School Development Plan.

Takeaways

- Students' assessment of their learning is subject to biases: hindsight, foresight and stability.
- There is a need to find a way that works for students to make realistic assessments of their own learning.

- Creating a culture of making mistakes as being excellent opportunities for learning is not easy but it would be brilliant and refreshing.
- Knowing how memory works can be taught to students, and will help them to assess what they know and how they know it.
- The best age to get into good learning habits is the primary schools age.

Homework

Have a go at answering these questions.

1. What is the problem with students' assessment of their learning?
2. What (generally) do students believe is the best way of learning?
3. Why is this?
4. What is retrieval fluency?
5. Can the skill of learning about learning be taught?

How would this help with test anxiety?

References

Agarwal, P. K., D'Antonio, L., Roediger, H. L., McDermott, K. B. & McDaniel, M. A. (2014). Classroom-based programs of retrieval practice reduce middle school and high school students' test anxiety. *Journal of Applied Research in Memory and Cognition*, 3(3), 131-139. https://doi.org/10.1016/j.jarmac.2014.07.002

Agarwal, P. K., Karpicke, J. D., Kang, S. H., Roediger, H. & McDermott, K. (2008). Examining the testing effect with open- and closed-book tests. *Applied Cognitive Psychology*, 22, 861-876. https://doi.org/10.1002/acp.1391

Bandura, A. (1997). *Self-efficacy. The exercise of control.* Stanford University, CA: W.H.Freeman/Times Books/Henry Holt & Co.

Bates, G. & Shea, J. (2024). Retrieval practice 'in the wild': Teachers' reported use of retrieval practice in the classroom. *Mind, brain, and education*, 18: 249-257. https://doi.org/10.1111/mbe.12420

Bjork, R. A. (1975). *Retrieval as a memory modifier: An interpretation of negative recency and related phenomena.* In R. L. Solso (ed.), *Information processing and cognition: The Loyola Symposium* (pp. 123-144). Mahwah, NJ: Lawrence Erlbaum. https://bjorklab.psych.ucla.edu/wp-content/uploads/sites/13/2016/07/RBjork_1975.pdf

Bjork, R. A. & Bjork, E. L. (2019). The myth that blocking one's study or practice by topic or skill enhances learning. In C. Barton (ed.), *Education myths: An evidence-informed guide for teachers.* Suffolk, UK: John Catt Educational Ltd. https://bjorklab.psych.ucla.edu/wp-content/uploads/sites/13/2020/01/BjorkBjorkEducatinMythChapterPublishedFormSept2019.pdf

Bjork, R. A. Dunlosky, J. & Kornell, N. (2013). Self-regulated learning: Beliefs, techniques and illusions. *Annual Review of Psychology*, 64, 417-44. https://doi.org/10.1146/annurev-psych-113011-143823

DeWinstanley, P. A. & Bjork, E. L. (2004). Processing strategies and the generation effect: Implications for making a better reader. *Memory & Cognition*, 32(6), 945-955. https://doi.org/10.3758/bf03196872

DfE https://www.gov.uk/government/publications/teachers-standards

Fischhoff, B. (1975). Hindsight is not equal to foresight: The effect of outcome knowledge on judgment under uncertainty. *Journal of Experimental Psychology: Human Perception and Performance*, 1(3), 288-299. https://doi.org/10.1037/0096-1523.1.3.288

Hattie, J. & Yates, G. Visible learning (2014). *Visible learning and the science of how we learn.* Abingdon, UK: Routledge.

Lipowski, S. L., Pyc, M. A., Dunlosky, J. & Rawson, K. A. (2014). Establishing and explaining the testing effect in free recall for young children. *Developmental Psychology, 50*(4), 994-1000. https://doi.org/10.1037/a0035202

Karpicke, J. D. & Roediger, H. K. (2008). The critical importance of retrieval for learning. *Science, 319*, 966-968. https://doi.org/10.1126/science.1152408

Koriat, A. & Bjork, R. A. (2006a). Illusions of competence during study can be remedied by manipulations that enhance learners' sensitivity to retrieval conditions at test. *Memory & Cognition, 34*(5), 959-972. https://doi.org/10.3758/bf03193244

Koriat, A. & Bjork, R. A. (2006b). Mending metacognitive illusions: A comparison of mnemonic-based and theory-based procedures. *Journal of Experimental Psychology: Learning, Memory and Cognition 2006, 32*(5),1133-1145. https://doi.org/10.1037/0278-7393.32.5.1133

Kornell, N. & Bjork, R. A. (2008). Learning concepts and categories: Is spacing the 'enemy of induction?' *Psychological Science, 19*(6), 585-592. https://doi.org/10.1111/j.1467-9280.2008.02127.x

Kornell, N. & Bjork, R. A. (2009). A stability bias in human memory: Overestimating remembering and underestimating learning. *Journal of Experimental Psychology: General, 138*(4). https://doi.org/10.1037/a0017350

McNamara D. S. (2010). Strategies to read and learn: Overcoming learning by consumption. *Medical Education, 44*(4), 340-346. https://pubmed.ncbi.nlm.nih.gov/20236240/

Pan, S. C. & Bjork, R. A. (2021). Acquiring a mental model of learning: Towards an owner's manual. In A. Wagner and M. Kahana (eds.), *Oxford handbook of learning and memory: Foundations and applications*. Oxford, UK: Oxford University Press.

Roediger, H. L. & Karpicke, J. D. (2011). Intricacies of spaced retrieval: A resolution. In A. S. Benjamin (ed.), *Successful remembering and successful forgetting: Essays in honor of Robert A. Bjork* (pp. 23-48). New York: Psychology Press.

Yan, V. X., Bjork, E. L. & Bjork, R.A. (2016). On the difficulty of mending metacognitive illusions: A priori theories, fluency effects, and misattributions of the interleaving benefit. *Journal of Experimental Psychology*: General 2016, *145*(7), 918-933. https://doi.org/10.1037/xge0000177

Yang, C., Luo, L., Vadillo, M. A., Yu, R. & Shanks, D. R. (2021). Testing (quizzing) boosts classroom learning: A systematic and meta-analytic review. *Psychological Bulletin.* Advance online publication. https://doi.org/10.1037/bul0000309

8 The Dream for Education
On the Soapbox

> **What to Expect**
>
> This chapter allows me to get it out of my system a little bit – the frustration about exams for exams' sake. The chapter also includes the Teacher Training Chunks for use in your setting. Finally, I share a little bit of the creative problem solving I've used in schools, for fun!

> **Key Terms**
>
> **cross-pollination of ideas:** how children can learn so many things if given the opportunity to be creative
>
> **SCAMPER:** **S**ubstitute, **C**ombine, **A**dapt, **M**odify, **P**ut to other uses, **E**liminate, **R**earrange/reverse – a problem-solving technique

Imagine an education where there were tests all the time but no high-stakes tests. The anxiety-producing evaluative situation that ensures you will not perform your best is a dim and distant memory – just gone. Imagine subject content that is not taught in blocks but is skills-based and far-reaching, comprising of many interesting subjects that are relevant to life today! This enables a student to draw on a thousand threads of knowledge to solve the problems in front of them that, globally, we so desperately need solving. Imagine the option to pursue subjects that you are interested in and motivated by, and choices that are not bound by what fits into a school timetable.

There has to be a more creative way?

The world has never travelled faster in terms of technological advances and will continue to do so. The job market has changed beyond recognition. It's no longer one job for life and many people hold multiple roles with a least one 'side hustle', yet the education system remains pretty much the same. It has not adapted to the outside world. Then how can we truly prepare our children for the future?

Given the vast swathes of information and the need to operate in global networks, the best education we can give our students is one that teaches them how to learn. The only reason we do not do this is because students have to take exams, so we are teaching to get them through exams. It's such a narrow tunnel of learning and experience.

A few weeks ago, I overheard some Year 10 girls (14–15 year olds):

Flossie: 'It feels like we just learn to take an exam so that we can take another exam.'

I could have cried.

I have long been an admirer of Ken Robinson (2011) who argues that schools educate children out of creativity. I am a fan of creative problem-solving and taught many students (and staff) over the years to SCAMPER (Isaksen et al., 2011). I admire the 'five minds' of Howard Gardner (2008): respecting, ethical, creating, disciplined and synthesising. I loved the 'Hole in the wall' TED Talk by Sugata Mitra. (I know it's old, but ask yourselves if anything has really changed since we were shown this inspiring idea?) Mitra's talk is a great example of how children can learn so many things if given the opportunity to be creative. A cross-pollination of ideas and skills. But we can't do a lot of this in schools, certainly not if Year 6 are taking SATs and Years 10 and 11 have GCSEs. All the *real* learning that we are 'insetted' about and feel inspired by has to sit by the wayside because of teaching content for the exam.

In a (Sad) Nutshell

As educators, we have a moral duty to the students in our care to develop their learning potential to its fullest capacity, yet we input information into students for an exam at the end of it an exam that a student doesn't even receive feedback from! All that hard work and study students put in for GCSEs and A levels and, at the end, they don't know what they know or don't know because there is no individual feedback. Simply, we are educating students to take exams (GCSEs) which are a passport to taking some subjects further that you may enjoy (but have to fit into a school timetable). World problems need solutions and I fear they won't be found because our education system teaches students to think in blocks of knowledge rather than cross-pollinating ideas.

Topic work in primary schools sets a good ground for cross-pollinating ideas, but the secondary school curriculum in the UK (GCSEs) takes away any creative thinking at a time when students' brains are firing on all cylinders. GCSEs are not helpful. There are so many creative ways we could bring students to A level or IB courses without sitting GCSEs. Reform is needed. It is long overdue. Some creative thinking about the future, please. Or just get rid of all the exams. Find a different, more creative way to educate for the future.

Tools at Your Disposal

The Scheme of Work in this book and the teacher training materials with the suggested School Development Plan could be integral to developing learning and improving outcomes for students. These resources come from the research that discusses judgements of learning (e.g. Bjork et al., 2013) and students' inability to judge what they know as well as the inescapable research about the testing effect. Moreover, these ideas came from wanting to help students who are crumbling with the thought of high-stakes tests. So, for as long as we remain in this system, we are compelled to help the students navigate it. That's what this book is for.

I suggest teaching students about memory and biases such as foresight bias and hindsight bias. In my opinion, if these learning how to learn (Bjork, 2014) techniques are embedded in a pastoral curriculum, then this provision would reduce the need for test anxiety. What better education could we give than actually teaching students how to learn?

There is a need to develop training for teachers (and parents) and curricula for students that build on the recent additions of desirable difficulties to the UK Initial Teacher Training framework (2020) and teach more about how memory works and the different learning biases of foresight and hindsight bias. There is a need to create an age-relative, year-upon-year learning skills incremental curriculum using desirable difficulties. You now have these resources and you can edit, change, discard, re-write … but I hope I have started the ball rolling. It's all there:

- the Scheme of Work for ages 9 (KS2–KS5 and beyond) upwards with all resources! (Chapter 6)
- the teacher training package (this chapter – coming up)
- the School Development Plan (Chapter 9)
- plus a lot information you can draw on in all these chapters …

Let's do it!

In A Nutshell

SCAMPER is a problem-solving technique (Isaksen et al., 2011). I used it to teach the poem 'The Highwayman' by Alfred Noyes in a Year 5 English class. We had fun by firstly identifying the problem: *Bess gets shot!* Then we worked in groups to **S**ubstitute, **C**ombine, **A**dapt, **M**odify, **P**ut to other uses, **E**liminate, **R**earrange/**R**everse. In this case, we worked with the narrative of this poem. The only thing to think about is to make sure the students know what these words mean – e.g. *Modify* is a small change. Then go to group presentations on this – e.g. *the ale was substituted with poison so that the guards all died and then Bess wasn't shot*. It's just fun to think in this way: mix it up, generate ideas, think out of the BLOCKS!

Teacher Training Programme and Roll Out in Desirable Difficulties to Control Test Anxiety.

The aim of the next few pages is to give you the information you need to be able to train teachers and parents in desirable difficulties, and be able to turn the information into a PowerPoint or presentation that uses this text for ease. Ultimately, the best thing is for a teacher who is going to roll out the PSHE/Pastoral Scheme of Work to have read this book. However, where that is not possible and knowing that time can be difficult to find in the school day, the following pages contain the *absolute key information* to share with teachers and parents, and could be placed in a series of PowerPoint slides or used in any other way. I have tried to chunk the key information for use as you wish and in a reproduceable form, but in the order that is best.

The following are just suggestions to help you reach as wide an audience as possible with as much ready information as possible.

Chunk 1/Slide 1: Giving Back Control

There is some ground-breaking research which shows that giving students back more control over their learning can reduce anxiety about taking tests.

At least 10–20% of any classroom will have students who are anxious about taking high-stakes tests. The research used a method for revision and an intervention that now provides us with a new PSHE/Pastoral Scheme of Work that we will deliver to all students, as it's great for promoting overall wellbeing too. This works by teaching the students *how* they learn – *how* memory works – so that if they test themselves rather than re-reading or highlighting as they revise, and if they allow some forgetting to set in (they study but don't test straightaway; they do that two days later), they will eventually be able to recall this even if they are feeling anxious. We will teach them that by studying in this way 'their testing routes are well-oiled'.

Chunk 2/Slide 2: Desirable Difficulties

The method of revision is to use desirable difficulties (Bjork, 1975) and, in particular, the testing effect or retrieval practice that became a mandatory requirement in the Teaching Standards from 2020. The desirable difficulties are:

- varying conditions of practice
- spacing study or practice sessions
- interleaving vs blocking
- generation and using tests – *the testing effect (retrieval practice)*.

What do you understand by these terms? (Getting you to think about this before we input or tell you the information is a really effective way to cue the information into your memories. We are not robots, and we can't input information and expect output – memory likes elaboration and cues. Memory likes mistakes!)

Where are these conditions practised in your current school environment?

Where could they be used in your current educational setting?

Chunk 3/Slide 3: Varying Conditions of Practice

Varying conditions of practice means that you might change the place where you study (recall) (Imundo et al.,2020). You may go outside, or you may take the students to a coffee shop and recall information there. It is useful, if possible, to take students to the exam room where they will take the tests and if this includes individual rooms for students with individual needs then they should be afforded the same opportunities. So there are some logistics to encounter here, but this may really help students who feel anxious about taking exams.

However, varying conditions of practice does not just mean changing the room. If you are a teacher that always uses a multiple-choice quiz, change this at times. Varying conditions of practice means just that: lots of different variations of input and recalling of material (although the best recall for long-term memory has been shown to be writing short answers, so not multiple-choice but a couple of sentences that explain the answer to a question). There is no evidence base to merit including learning-style assessments in education (Pashler et al., 2009). This sounds harsh, I know. It feels counterintuitive for teachers to not cater to preferred learning styles. After all, for many years we have been told that we should/must. For many of you out there, you will have been through the VAK – visual, audio and kinesthetic mantras, a plethora of other training sessions on preferred learning styles. Research actually suggests that because memory likes cues, then if you're having to work hard or struggle to understand – in other words, learn outside of your comfort zone – you may actually remember more. The myth of learning styles de-bunked. As the great authors of *Make it stick* (Brown et al., 2014, p. 9) say: 'When the learning is harder it's stronger and lasts longer.'

A note of caution is needed with regard to students with individual learning needs as in many cases their provision cannot be altered. There is some research, though, that suggests retrieval practice; the testing effect (testing) is an effective method to use with students with low working memory scores (Agarwal et al., 2017).

Copyright material from Helen Barsham (2026) *Supporting Children and Young People With Test Anxiety*, Routledge

Chunk 4/Slide 4: Spacing Study or Practice Sessions/Distributed Practice

Bjork (1975) talks about these. Bjork and Bjork (2011) also credit spacing as having a great and significant impact on learning. Dunlosky et al. (2013) conducted a comprehensive survey on the effectiveness of ten different learning techniques. Typically, observed student techniques such as re-reading, highlighting, keyword mnemonics, summarization and imagery use for text learning were found to have low usefulness, whereas retrieval practice or testing and distributed (spaced) practice were found to be highly useful. The point is to let some forgetting set in. That is why the timing of the initial test is important. Testing directly after reading or re-reading or restudying (study, study, study, test) can lead to incorrect metacognition about the material that has been learned because it is easy to recall. This is the bias of retrieval fluency. 'I did well on a test, so I know this.'

Chunk 5/Slide 5: Interleaving vs Blocking – The Testing Effect

One of the best examples of this is given in the book *Make it stick* (Brown et al., 2014) with the example about teaching baseball at 'Cal Poly' (read pages 79-82).

What is this saying about blocked or massed practice vs interleaving? Take responses.

Essentially, if you practice the same thing – in this case, a fixed-length throw over and over again – you will be the best at that particular throw when tested a week later. However, if you practice different distances and interleave them, you won't be the best a week later, but you will be the best at that stroke six weeks later. Moreover, you will have the better throws all round at all the different distances. Interleaving and spacing takes longer to master but the knowledge is stronger and lasts longer.

You can demonstrate this with staff by using little bean-bag throws. One group practises one distance and the other group practises three distances. Then ask: *Who is better after one week?* and *Who is better after 6 weeks?*

The testing effect or retrieval practice

'Study, test, test, test' is 150% more effective in terms of retaining knowledge in memory than 'study, study, study, test' or 'study, test, study, test, study, test'. It's harder to recall though, it's effortful, and students prefer to re-read and highlight and cram for tests (see arguments about blocking). Students should:

- study something, then
- test themselves two days later, and
- look up or take feedback on what they got wrong (making mistakes is excellent for cues into memory),
- then test themselves again two days later.

They should not block their subjects but mix them up and space their testing out (see the optimal testing/revision schedule in Chapter 3).

True Story in Actions: Changing How We Teach Spellings

First, we had to warn a group of primary school parents who we were coming away from getting stars etc. for 20/20 spellings, as we're learning how to learn to spell for life and not just for a test. As an English teacher, I had performed the weekly spelling test dutifully for many years. So, the students learn a spelling pattern and are then tested on that pattern. Then a piece of writing will follow and the words that had been spelt correctly for the test were often spelt incorrectly in the writing. This is because they had been blocked or crammed for the spelling test, but the learning was not then applied to the wider context of writing.

So, we started to mix up the testing and test week 6 with week 3, or week 4 and week 2 and so on, and the results were not as good! However, feedback on the correct spellings was given every time and, when the spelling was eventually learned, it was never forgotten because it was in the long-term memory. Learning for life not just a spelling test. This was the way spellings were taught in the 1920s (Horn & Ashbaugh, 1920).

Copyright material from Helen Barsham (2026) *Supporting Children and Young People With Test Anxiety*, Routledge

Chunk 6: Some Extra Tips

Remember that testing yourself on something you don't know is an excellent way to prime your brain to receive the new knowledge (Giebl et al., 2020).

- Do a test on the material and *then* learn the material – the brain or memory has cues and hooks it can pin the knowledge on by doing it this way.
- Test yourself in the exam room itself, if you can.
- Practise the art of memory palaces. Place your knowledge round the coffee shop; for example, imagine your list of information about photosynthesis is by the coffee beans or the functions of the heart by the toilet door, and then just remember the place – and the list will come to you.
- Use other mnemonics. Many memory athletes – those that can memorize the order of a whole pack of cards or two packs, or some such feats, often use imagery. Some use rude imagery to help them.

Study periods are recall periods – so why not name them so on the school timetable?

NB

Never ever forget that every time you recall the information (once you have let some forgetting set in), *it becomes easier to recall*. If you prepare for important exams in this way, your 'testing routes will be well-oiled' and, even if you *are* anxious about exams, you will have the information available to you.

Chunk 7: More Extra Tips

- If you practice interleaving knowledge, it is more difficult during initial acquisition of the information but improves learning over the long term.
- Interleaving and retrieval practice naturally give more errors, and these are learning opportunities – failure to retrieve correctly yields better memory (corrective feedback) (Kornell et al., 2009).
- The benefits of retrieval practice are greater for students with lower working memory capacity (Agarwal et al., 2017).
- Effortful retrieval (the testing effect) is a powerful mnemonic device and improves later retention on tested material (Roediger & Karpicke 2006a, 2006b, 2008).
- The best type of testing is short-answer recall.
- Students make suboptimal choices (Dirkx et al., 2019) due to core existing beliefs in the superiority of blocked practice (it feels easier).
- Interleaving and retrieval practice naturally give more errors, and these are learning opportunities: failure to retrieve correctly yields better memory (corrective feedback needed) (Kornell et al., 2009)
- Benefits of retrieval practice are greater for students with lower working memory (Agarwal et al., 2017)
- Incorrect retrievals can become hypercorrections – great learning events – as long as feedback given. For example, if you are delivering an important speech and you make a mistake and you have hundreds of people listening, you are unlikely to ever forget this event or what you were saying.

TIP: Make sure you understand these biases before you share them.

Finally – Chunk 8: Forgetting

Forgetting is one of the most misunderstood aspects of learning. The harder it is to remember something, the more likely you will remember it in the long term, once remembered or recalled.

Feedback is critical. Learning by making a mistake but then finding out the correct answer is powerful learning.

Testing yourself every two days and mixing up the information is a powerful way to input information – every time you recall it, you can more easily recall it when needed.

We are all subject to learning biases:

- foresight bias
- hindsight bias, and
- fluency bias.

What do you think these terms mean?

And if you'd like to know more, here is a list of references that are just about retrieval practice and the best ways to study, so that you can see the resources I have drawn on.

References

Agarwal, P. K., Finley, J. R., Rose, N. S. & Roediger, H. L., 3rd (2017). Benefits from retrieval practice are greater for students with lower working memory capacity, *Memory 25*(6), 764–771. https://doi.org/10.1080/09658211.2016.1220579

Bjork, R. A. (1975). Retrieval as a memory modifier: An interpretation of negative recency and related phenomena. In R. L. Solso (ed.), *Information processing and cognition: The Loyola Symposium* (pp. 123–144). Hillsdale, NJ: Erlbaum.

Bjork, E. L. & Bjork, R. A. (2011). Making things hard on yourself, but in a good way: Creating desirable difficulties to enhance learning. In M. A. Gernsbacher, R. W. Pew & J. R. Pomerantz (eds.), *Psychology and the real world: Essays illustrating fundamental contributions to society* (pp. 56–64). New York: Worth Publishers.

Bjork, R. A., Dunlosky, J. & Kornell, N. (2013). Self-regulated learning: Beliefs, techniques and illusions. *Annual Review of Psychology, 64*, 417–444. doi: 10.1146/annurev-psych-113011-143823

Bjork, R. A. (2014, March 30) Learning to learn. Conversation with Bob Bjork (Part 1) YouTube [video] https://www.youtube.com/watch?v=fTtbp6TyBrI

Brown, P. C., Roediger, H. L. & McDaniel, M. A. (2014) *Make it stick, the science of successful learning.* Cambridge, MA: Belknap Press, Harvard University Press. https://doi.org/10.1080/00220671.2015.1053373

Dirkx, K. J. H., Camp, G., Kester, L., Kirschner & P. A. (2019). Do secondary students make use of effective study strategies when they study on their own? *Applied Cognitive Psychology, 33*(5) 952–957. https://doi.org/10.1002/acp.3584

Dunlosky, J., Rawson, K. A., Marsh, E. J., Nathan, M. J. & Willingham, D.T. (2013) Improving students' learning with effective learning techniques: Promising directions from cognitive and educational psychology. *Psychological Science in the Public Interest, 14*(1): 4–58. doi: 10.1177/1529100612453266. PMID: 26173288

Gardner, H. (2008) *Five minds for the future.* Boston, MA: Harvard Business Press.

Giebl, S., Mena, S., Storm, B. C., Bjork, E. L. & Bjork, R. A. (2020). Answer first or Google first? Using the internet in ways that enhance, not impair, one's subsequent retention of needed information. *Psychology Learning & Teaching, 20*(1), 58–75. https://doi.org/10.1177/1475725720961593 (original work published 2021).

Horn, E. & Ashnaugh, E.J. (1920). *Lippincott's Horn: Ashbaugh speller for grades 1-8*. Salt Lake City, UT: Project Gutenberg.

Imundo, M. N., Pan, S. C., Bjork, E. L. & Bjork, R. A. (2020). Where and how to learn: The interactive benefits of contextual variation, restudying, and retrieval practice for learning. *Quarterly Journal of Experimental Psychology* https://doi.org/10.1177/1747021820968483

Isaksen, S. G., Dorval, K. B. & Treffinger, D. J. (2011). *Creative approaches to problem solving*. London; LA; New Delhi; Singapore; Washington, DC: SAGE.

Karpicke, J. D. & Roediger III H. L. (2007). Repeated retrieval during learning is the key to long-term retention. *Journal of Memory and Language, 57*, 151-162. doi:10.1016/j/jml.2006.09.004

Karpicke, J. D. & Roediger III, H. K. (2008). The critical importance of retrieval for learning. *Science, 319*, 966-968. doi: 10.1126/science.1152408

Kornell, N. & Bjork, R. A. (2009). A stability bias in human memory: Overestimating remembering and underestimating learning. *Journal of Experimental Psychology: General, 138*(4). https://doi.org/10.1037/a0017350

Kornell, N., Hays, M. J. & Bjork, R. A. (2009). Unsuccessful retrieval attempts enhance subsequent learning. *Psychology: Learning, Memory, and Cognition, 35*(4): 989-998. doi: 10.1037/a0015729

Kornell, N., Klein, P. J. & Rawson, K. A. (2015). Retrieval attempts enhance learning, but retrieval success (versus failure) does not matter. *Journal of Experimental Psychology: Learning, Memory, and Cognition, 41*(1), 283-294. doi:org/10.1037/a0037850

Mitra, Sugata *Hole in the Wall* TED Talk https://www.ted.com/talks/sugata_mitra_kids_can_teach_themselves?language=en Pashler, H., McDaniel, M., Rohrer, D. & Bjork, R. (2009). Learning styles: Concepts and evidence. *Psychological Science in the Public Interest, 9*(3), 105-119. https://doi.org/10.1111/j.1539-6053.2009.01038.x (original work published 2008).

Robinson, K. (2011). *Out of our minds: Learning to be creative*. Chichester: Capstone Publishing.

Roediger III, H. L. & Karpicke, J. D. (2006a). Test-enhanced learning: Taking memory tests improves long-term retention. *Psychological Science, 17*, 249-255.

Roediger III, H. L. & Karpicke J. D. (2006b). The power of testing memory. Basic research and implications for educational practice. *Perspectives on Psychological Science, 1*, 181-210. doi: 10.1111/j.1745-6916.2006.00012.x 1

Roediger III, H. L. & Karpicke J. D. (2008). The critical importance of retrieval for learning. *Science, 319*, 966-968. doi:10.1126/science.1152408

Roediger, H. L., Aggarwal, P. K., McDaniel, M. A. & McDermott, K. B. (2011). Test enhanced learning in the classroom: Long term improvements from quizzing. *Journal of Experimental Psychology, 17*(4): 382-395. doi: 10.1037/a0026252

9 School Development Plan to Give Students Back Control for Taking Exams

> **What to Expect**
>
> This chapter includes the suggestions for embedding good practice concerning the wellbeing of students around taking tests. This comes in the form of a suggested Whole School Development Plan.

> **Key Terms**
>
> **academic/pastoral/marketing/CPD/performance management:** this stuff needs to be everywhere!
> **attributional training** (for teachers)**:** to help manage feedback
> **audit:** how feedback is given around exams
> **senior management team (SMT) agenda:** to allow time every week to dedicate to managing test anxiety

School Development Plan to Give Students Back Control for Taking Exams

The PSHE/Pastoral Scheme of Work in Chapter 6 should be delivered *at least once in a key stage* and there is the opportunity to *mix and match at will*. Delivered as standalones as part of a PSHE/Pastoral curriculum, the lessons are a powerful tool for helping students take back control when taking high-stakes tests. The key is in enabling students to understand how memory works. However, a whole-school approach is needed to give students back control, and not just a six/seven week Scheme of Work.

Soapbox: *Until we reach such a time that there is major educational reform in the UK and the boxy system of GCSEs etc. is altered, we have a moral responsibility to help students navigate these trying tests.*

From an early age, the perception of a test is not one of a test being a learning experience. While this may be changing now with the introduction of retrieval practice into the teaching standards, I suggest that the majority of teachers reading this book have heard on one, if not more, occasions students bemoaning the fact that they have a test in Religious Education, Biology, Maths, etc. Tests are viewed as hurdles to leap rather than learning opportunities. We need to reach a status quo whereby if someone asks a child what the purpose of testing is they will say 'recall aids recall', and 'it's for getting information into the long-term memory', and 'interleaving and spacing make recall harder, which makes the learning stronger', as opposed to 'they want to torture us', 'so we can compare how we're doing with our friends', or 'they want to know how well we're doing'.

To enact this shift in attitude, major curriculum reform would help. However, in the absence of that, here is a potential, suggested whole-school development plan that might serve as a great whole-school initiative for a prospective/current school leader to undertake to deliver – someone embarking on the National Professional Qualification for Senior Leadership (NPQSL)/National Professional Qualification for Headship (NPQH) programmes, perhaps.

Teaching Standard 2/8 requires pupils to retrieve information from memory, and spacing practice so that pupils who revisit ideas after a gap are also likely to strengthen recall.

Back to Feedback

It will be critical to start with **feedback.** How do you do it? What is good about it? How do teachers feed back after a test? What can be improved? How do you manage peer comparison? Do teachers/parents/peers use fear appeals (Chapter 2)?

The activities, stages and roles assigned in the following are simply guidelines, as each setting will be unique. I hope you can see how to make this work and how useful this could be in helping students to gain some control over taking tests.

School Development Plan: Activities and Stages for Giving Students Back Control in Taking High Stakes Tests

Stage	Activity
Stage 1	• **Initial INSET:** the lead should be whomever is taking the lead in this whole transformative process – a person or persons with the 'buy in'. This person could be in leadership but doesn't have to be. What is important is that they do not feel this has all been 'last minute' and that they have not had time to prepare properly. • (Mixed staff groups – mix departments – year groups – just get a good mixture.) **Ask questions:** Q: How do different teachers manage testing? Do they use fear appeals? If staff have not heard of these – it's OK – explain that you want them to think what they may be. Q: How do students feel about taking tests in their school setting? Q: Are there problems with peer comparison? How are test results given back to students? **Ask for feedback:** Ask each group to feed back on these questions.

Copyright material from Helen Barsham (2026) *Supporting Children and Young People With Test Anxiety*, Routledge

Stage	Activity
	Research: Introduce research on: • fear appeals • test anxiety • desirable difficulties.
Stage 2	• **Senior management team (STM):** to have a regular agenda item on 'giving back students control over testing'. • **In the first meeting:** discuss feedback from the INSET session, what the implications for their setting are and how they will tweak this plan to fit their school setting. • **Draft:** start to draft this section for pupil wellbeing into the Schools' Development/Improvement plan. This applies to primary/secondary and further education settings.
Stage 3	**SMT meeting agenda items to include:** • **marketing** – what can you put on your website/media channels about how you are giving students back control? • **in-school media messages** – how can you mirror the content of the PSHE/Pastoral Scheme of Work throughout the school and how will you display? For example, if you have a TV, can you have a key message from 'desirable difficulties' up there every week such as *'study, test, test, test is 150% more effective than study, study, study, test'*? **Questions for pastoral lead/CPD:** • How, when and with whom are you going to use the 'desirable difficulties' training and then the PSHE/Pastoral Scheme of Work? • When will you deliver the PSHE/Pastoral Scheme of Work? (It should be six weeks before any high-stakes exams) • Who is going to deliver the programme for the different year groups? When will they have time to read/train on the materials? • To what extent can you train up the whole staff? Do you start with a small group and go via year teams/departments? • How will you organize planning agendas of future inset and staff meetings to cover all aspects of test anxiety and desirable difficulties so that more staff are trained in this? • Who is leading on the parent engagement? • Who will provide a programme of attributional training for teachers so they can manage feedback from tests more effectively? Do you have funds to bring in training for this? Who can take on attribution theory and disseminate? This could be really transformative in terms of giving feedback for staff and hugely improve students' experience. Can assemblies on these themes be delivered? **Questions for the SMT:** • Do all staff know about test anxiety? • Fear appeals? • And desirable difficulties? **NB:** Remember to note any changes, pastoral or academic, in school policies.

Stage	Activity
	Questions about Parent Lead: • Do you have one? • How can you get your messages across to parents? Run parents' evenings, or recorded Zoom/webinars? • Can you invite to school assemblies on test anxiety/sesirable difficulties? **Questions about Academic Lead:** • Can *study periods* be renamed as *recall periods*? • What else needs to be done by the academic team to ensure success of this programme? • How can you appoint a 'study, test, test, test' students' champion. • How will you change the culture of the school so that testing is seen as a positive rather than a negative? • What can you do around feedback/attributional training? • On learning walks and in lesson observations are you seeing desirable difficulties? Are fear appeals being used? • Who is engaging parents? **Question for Deputy Head/Head:** • Do line management targets to include desirable difficulties? • How will you monitor and maximise the impact of the PSHE/Pastoral Scheme of Work? • How will you evaluate the impact of this part of the School Development Plan? • Who is engaging parents? **Questions for CPD Lead:** • How will you plan agendas of future inset and staff meetings to cover all aspects of test anxiety and desirable difficulties so that more staff are trained in this? • How will you implement a programme of attributional training for teachers so that they can manage feedback from tests more effectively? **NB:** Remember to note any changes pastoral or academic in school policies.
Stage 4	**Review of actions taken so far. What else is needed?**

Reference

DfE https://www.gov.uk/government/publications/teachers-standards

10 In Conclusion

It's been a rollercoaster! We started with a brief guide to what test anxiety is and then looked at what is happening around students when 'Fear Appeals' are used. Chapter 3 was a biggy as it included the research about 'Desirable Difficulties'! It's natural to look at how students monitor their learning after this and the biases that can creep in so we moved to knowledge biases here too. Chapter 4 was about the concept of self-efficacy in test taking and the golden thread of the book, which is about trying to give students back control in evaluative situations. Chapter 5 brought extra information that didn't really belong in any category and then I got practical. Chapter 6 is the intervention or, as it is now – in its new form – a fully differentiated Scheme of Work for PHSE or PASTORAL time for Years 4 through to Year 13. Chapter 7 brought things back to theory and more on how we can encourage students to monitor their own learning, and Chapter 8 is where I took a breather and just got some of my ideas and passions 'out there' plus the practical suggestions for content in 'chunks' for teacher training/parent training PowerPoints. Chapter 9 is an idea, a brief School Development Plan to help settings in making the wellbeing of their students around exams a core purpose rather than a tick-box exercise.

Back at the start, I may have lost some of you when I talked about getting parental engagement first. It's important that we try. Also, I may have lost some of you when you thought about the standards, curricula and test demands you are held to at KS2, 4 and 5 and I was writing about learning to learn, not learning for tests. I hope you still read this book. I know the challenges of a busy school and the tiredness teachers and leaders battle, but I also know how much you care about the 'kids'. I have been lucky enough to work with many heroes over my long career (you know who you are!) and it never ceases to amaze me just how wonderfully giving you are of yourselves and your time for young people. Here's a shout out to those heroes out there.

Talking of those wonderful young people, I have written a separate guidebook for them about self-efficacy in test taking, how to recall using Desirable Difficulties, etc., and I did let them know that I am asking teachers to think about the 'revving up' at exam points of the year and the use of Fear Appeals. 'Manage Test Anxiety' is a student guide available from Triggerhub Publishing.

I restrained myself with the soapbox but there has to be a bit of give? Writing a book is hard work and a long process, and I do feel so passionately for the kids who are 'taking one exam so that they can take another exam'.

As I said, the doctorate was inspired by students who were taking high-stakes tests who were just feeling overwhelmed. The research, this book is my promise to them that I would try to make a real difference. It is applicable to everyone who is involved in taking (setting) high stakes tests (from Year 6 upwards). I wanted to create something tangible that would help. We contextualize and relate classroom learning to anything that helps get our messages across but we rarely (I think) spend the time explaining how memory works for tests.

I was once accused of being 'too enthusiastic' in a school setting. That is my passion for wanting the best education for students (and teachers) coming through. I understand that enthusiasm can be annoying and I am a bit 'tigger-like', but that enthusiasm has delivered the research and the book (no mean feat) and I hope will support all the stakeholders, especially the students and those who fear taking tests, in your school or setting.

Maybe some of you are inspired by this book and can't wait to get going? I hope you feel you have the necessary tools to do so. If you ever wanted more input or a chat you can contact me: helen@fighttestanxiety.com. Web: fighttestanxiety.com

The **most important takeaway** is that by teaching your students how memory learns for tests, that 'study, test, test, test', as a way to revise, will store knowledge needed for an exam, in the long-term memory, and revising in this way and reminding yourself how you have studied (to put knowledge into the long-term memory) reduces anxiety about exams. **The only thing your students need to remember is that their 'testing routes are well oiled' because 'recall aids recall'. Just this will help ...**

Soapbox – last one: Maybe if enough people can wave the problem of test anxiety under the nose of the Government and Education Departments, there will be a reform around tests, especially the GCSEs, and a new, innovative and creative system of education established, in its place, that truly prepares our young people for life today. If this dream came to pass – this book would not be needed, and I really wouldn't mind that at all. As I typed that, the Independent Curriculum and Assessment Review published their interim report. To comment on that needs another book but before they produce another report, I hope they read this one!

'study, test, test, test'

The Final Nitty Gritty

Teach students to learn how to learn and do this in the primary as well as secondary phases, but start early in primary.

- Teach them how memory works for tests.
- Get them to recall. Make a mantra: 'My testing routes are well oiled.' Recall aids recall.
- Deliver the intervention (PSHE/PASTORAL Scheme of Work) so that students know about the testing effect, interleaving, spacing and learning biases.
- Think about blocking. One more O in this word and you have a good expletive for how I feel about kids taking tests for the sake of them!

- Embed a test-taking, no worries about mistakes, culture in school from an early age.
- Train students, teachers and parents (and the DfE?) in Desirable Difficulties.
- Stop using Fear Appeals, if you do. Think what else you can do at exam time to ease the whole feeling of SILENCE/EXAM IN PROGRESS.
- Audit how you're feeding back around tests. How do you students feel? How are staff managing this?

Appendix A

Children's Test Attitude Questionnaires (English Version)

Children's Test Anxiety Scale

The 'check the time' question has been missed out. Also, the title includes the word 'attitude' rather than 'anxiety' to avoid any priming.

Please answer the questions using the following numbers:

1 = almost never
2 = some of the time
3 = most of the time
4 = almost always

1. While I am taking tests I wonder if I will pass. _____
2. While I am taking tests my heart beats fast. _____
3. While I am taking tests I look around the room. _____
4. While I am taking tests I feel nervous. _____
5. While I am taking tests I think I'm going to get a bad result. _____
6. While I am taking tests it's hard for me to remember the answers. _____
7. While I am taking tests I play with my pen/pencil. _____
8. While I am taking tests my face feels hot. _____
9. While I am taking tests I worry about failing. _____
10. While I am taking tests my belly feels funny. _____
11. While I am taking tests I worry about doing something wrong. _____
12. While I am taking tests I think about what my result will be. _____

Copyright material from Helen Barsham (2026) *Supporting Children and Young People With Test Anxiety*, Routledge

13. While I am taking tests I find it hard to sit still. _____
14. While I am taking tests I wonder if my answers are right. _____
15. While I am taking tests I think I should have studied more. _____
16. While I am taking tests my head hurts. _____
17. While I am taking tests I look at other people. _____
18. While I am taking tests I think most of my answers are wrong. _____
19. While I am taking tests I feel warm. _____
20. While I am taking tests I worry about how hard the test is. _____
21. While I am taking tests I try to finish quickly. _____
22. While I am taking tests my hand shakes. _____
23. While I am taking tests I think about what will happen if I fail. _____
24. While I am taking tests I have to go to the bathroom. _____
25. While I am taking tests I tap my feet. _____
26. While I am taking tests I think about how badly I am doing. _____
27. While I am taking tests I feel scared. _____
28. While I am taking tests I worry about what my parents will say. _____
29. While I am taking tests I stare. _____

Shared courtesy of Doug Wren with his personal permission. Many thanks Doug!

Appendix B

The Children's Test Anxiety Questionnaire (CTAS)
(Wren & Benson, 2004)

How Confident Are You?

1 = I never do this
2 = I do this sometimes
3 = I do this many times
4 = I always do this

1. If I find a test hard, I keep trying. _____
2. If I find a test hard, I still feel confident in my ability to pass. _____
3. If I did badly on a test, I still feel positive about other tests. _____
4. If I find a test hard, I feel I will not pass. _____
5. When I take tests, I feel anxious about being in a different room to my usual classroom. _____
6. When I take tests, I feel anxious about the instructor. _____
7. If I find a test hard, I can't control negative thoughts about failing. _____
8. If I find a test hard, I start to doubt my ability to pass. _____
9. In tests, I panic if I see people finishing before me. _____
10. I can concentrate in tests, even if I find them difficult. _____
11. I enjoy taking tests. _____
12. I can remain cheerful about life, even if a test is hard. _____
13. I can manage in tests, even if I feel tired or unwell. _____
14. I understand that even if I find a test difficult, it is not the end of the world. _____
15. I don't worry about taking tests. _____

Questionnaire created by Dr. Helen Barsham

INDEX

Note: For figure citations, page numbers appear in *italics*. For table citations, page numbers appear in **bold**.

A Levels (Advanced General Certificate in Education) 2, 35, 44, 118, 126
academic buoyancy 62, 72
academic lead 141; suggestions for 50
academic management 138
access arrangements 13, 66, 76
Agarwal, P. K. 29, 31, 41, 53, 73, 120
agoraphobia 26
algebra 42, 116
anxiety 5-6
apathy 19
AQA (Assessment and Qualifications Alliance) 22
arousal theory 2
attentional theory 2
attic brain *39*
attribution theory 140
attributional training *see* training
audit: definition 138
autonomic reactions 12
Aveyard, B. 6, 61, 72

Bandura, A. 6, 59
baseball 37, 42, 116, 133
Bates, G. 118
Beano, The 39
Beilock, S. L. 75, 108
benefits of testing 109
Benson, J. 11
bereavement 63
bias 121-2; definition 115; *see also* foresight bias; hindsight bias; knowledge biases; stability bias
biology *39, 40,* 55, 96, 139
Bjork, E. 34, 42, 109, 111, 116-17, 120, 132
Bjork, R. 6, 31, 34, 36, 41-2, 48, 53, 95, 103-4, 106, 109, 111, 116-21, 132
blanket fear appeals *see* fear appeals

blanket intervention: definition 71
blocked conditioning 117
blocked practice 42, 45-7, 115
blocked teaching 62
blocking 68, 71, 90-1, 108-9, 116, 143; definition 33, 115; desirable difficulties 34-5, 41-3, 49, 54; interleaving *vs* 133; self-efficacy 62
blocks: definition of 22; of education 35
brain attic 48, 111-12, 122
brain freeze 7
brain plasticity 72, 75; definition 71
BTech exams 2, 44
bullying 17
Butler, A. C. 53

Cambridge National qualifications 44
capability, beliefs in 6, 20
chemistry *39, 40,* **52**
Children's Test Anxiety Questionnaire (CTAS) 11-12, 27, 82-4, 147 (App B)
Children's Test Anxiety Scale 103, 108, 145-6 (App A)
Children's Test Attitude Questionnaires 82, 145-6 (App A)
climate of testing 28
cognitive control 72
cognitive science 72
cognitive scientists 94-6, 104; discussion on learning 95-9; in conversation 89-91
cognitive test anxiety, reduction of 72-3
college: terminology *xiii*
computer-assisted instruction 61
Confidence Questionnaire 12, 60-1
confidence-boosting 75
contextualization: exam anxiety 7; memory and tests 6-7; power of 5-6

Continuing Professional Development (CPD) *xiii*, 25, 138, 140-1
control 58; definition of 58; giving back *xiii, xiv*, 4-5; intervention and 29-30; lack of 62-3; perceived 1, 6, 61-2, *62*; of test anxiety 128; testing situations 61-2; wellbeing, negative effect on 62-3; *see also* desirable difficulties; uncertain control
coping skills 75
cortisol 11, 13, 63
Covid-19 pandemic 2, 10, 65
cramming 35, 41-2, 46-7, 49, 51-2, 54, 71, 91, 101, 104, 108-9, 117
Crassus 69
creativity 125-6
CRIME mnemonic 77
cross-curricula approach 36
cross-pollination 36, 54, 126; definition 33, 125
Csikzentmihalyi, M. 3
cues 94, 103, 108, 130-1
cultural change xiv
culture of testing 28; definition 22

Daly, A. L. 62
data: analysis 12-13; sharing 13-14; *see also* performance data 14-15
delayed initial recall 112
delayed re-study 112
desirable difficulties *xii, xiv*, 6, 16, 20, 33-55, 128, 130; definition 1, 33; effectiveness of 37; intervention 72, 81, 94, 103, 108; scenarios 50-1; self-efficacy 64, 66; spacing study 34-7; spelling rocks 34; testing effect 37; varying practice conditions 34
DeWinstanley, P. A. 106, 121
distal anxiety 3-4
distributed practice 132
disuse *see* new theory of disuse
documents 83, 85-6, 89-93, 95-102, 104-6, 109, 111-13
'dream' for education 125-36; tools and techniques 127
dual coding 51
Dunlosky, J. 31, 37, 95, 104-5, 132
Dweck, C. 88, 95

Early Career Teachers 9, 17
Early Years Foundation Stage (EYFS) 42
eating disorders 26
ecology 92-3
educational setting *xiii*
effort 6, 47-9
Effortful Educator blog/website 29, 108

effortful retrieval 47-8, 112, 118, 135
elaboration 94, 103, 108, 130
English language 5, 7, *39*, 40
enthusiasm 19, 143
evaluation anxiety 2
exams: definition *xiii*
executive functioning 3
executive processing 4-5
expectancy theory 2
extra tips 134-5

fear appeals *xii, xiv*, 3, 20, 22-32, 62; blanket 22, 24; current practice, audit of 30; definition 1, 24; intervention 29-30; personal experience 22-3; scenarios 25-8
feedback *xii, xiv*, 45, 52, 54, 65; corrective 135; critical nature of 53; school development plans 139, **139-41**; staff management of 14-15
feelings about exams 11
fight, flight or freeze modes 7, 38, *39*, 59, 74
flashcards 50, 51
fluency bias 136
foresight bias 41, 43, 48, 54, 122, 136; definition 106, 121
forgetting/forgetfulness 36, 48, 68, 136; benefits of 33
form teachers: suggestions for 51
free recall: definition 97; immediate tests 104
French *39*, 40
Functional Skills 44

Gardner, H. 126
GCSEs (General Certificate in Secondary Education) 1-2, 5, 7, 126, 138, 143; desirable difficulties 35-6, 40, 42, 44, 49, 52, 54; intervention 96, 103; metacognition of learning 118; self-efficacy 66
geography *39*, 40, **52**, 96
giving back control 80-113, 129; practical steps 7-8; strategies 113; *see also* intervention; school development plans
Google 29
growth mindset: assemblies 16; concept 68

Hattie, J. 68, 77, 109, 118
Hattie's Chunks 77
Hays, M. J. 53
head teachers, suggestions for 66-7, 141
Hendry, F. M.: *Chandra* 5
highlighting 37, 42, 49, 95, 109, 132

hindsight bias 43-4, 54, 121-2, 136; definition 106, 121
Hinton, S. E.: *The Outsiders* 5
history teachers: suggestions for 50-1
homework (for reader) 20; desirable difficulties 54-5; fear appeals 31; intervention 77; metacognition of learning 123; self-efficacy 67
hypercorrection 96

imagery 37; use of 132, 134
in-school media messages 140
Independent Curriculum and Assessment Review 143
Initial Teacher Training Core Framework 29
INSET (In-Service Training) 14-15, 18, 49, 67, 139-40
interleaving 94, 103, 108-9, 135, 139; benefits of 42, 116-17; blocking vs 133; definition 100; desirable difficulties 36-7, 42, 49, **52**; spelling tests 46; theory of 117
International Baccalaureate (IB) 2, 44, 126
intervention *xiv*, 2, 71-7; benefits of 76; blanket 49, 71, 73; to control test anxiety 29-30; definition 1, 71; delivery, ease of 80-2; effectiveness of 72; giving back control 80-113; learning goals 81-2; research, lack of 72; writing tasks 75
Izawa, C. 52-3

JCQ (Joint Council for Qualifications) 5, 18, 23, 66
journalling 75
judgements of learning 33, 35, 42, 54, 108-9; definition 115; incorrect 115-16

Karpicke, J. 31, 40, 42, 95, 97-8, 109, 116
knowledge: biases *xiv*, 33, 41-4, **44**, 46; recall 39, 40; understanding of 116-18
Koriat, A. 119
Kornell, N. 41, 53, 117, 119

Lang, J. 75
Lang, J. W. B. 75
languages 69
learned helplessness 28
learning biases 103, 106, 119
Learning Scientists blog/website 29, 108
learning: judgements of 109; 'learning to learn' as a critical survival tool 120-1; modes of 104-5; monitoring of 122
Liebert, R. 4
Likert scales 11-12
Lipowski, S. L. 109, 122

loci system 68
low working memory 44, 73, 131, 135; definition 71
Luo, L. 29, 53

Make it Stick (Brown, et al., 2014) 31, 34, 37, 133
maladaptive interaction 3
'Manage Test Anxiety' (Triggerhub Publishing) 142
marketing 67, 138
Marsh, E. J. 53
massed practice 42, 68, 109, 116
material: definition 97
mathematics 39, 40, 96, 139
Matthews, G. 2-4, 58
McKeachie, W. J. 75-6
McNamara, D. S. 109, 118
measuring test anxiety 13
memory 20, 95, 103; ancient 68-9; chunking ideas 68; contextualization 6-7; forgetting and 68; long-term 69, 74, 81, 104, 111, 133, 139; unknown content 41; *see also* low-working memory; memory hotspots; memory modifiers; memory palaces
memory hotspots *xiii*, 20; desirable difficulties 55; fear appeals 31-2; intervention 77; self-efficacy 68-9
memory modifiers 53
memory palaces 31-2, 55, 64, 134
mental health 25, 63
metacognition of learning *xiv*, 6, 33, 40-3, **43**, 81, 115-23; definition 80; monitoring 115, 119-20; promotion of **44**; solutions for improvements to 119
mistakes, making 43, 109, 115, 117, 122-3
Mithridates 69
Mitra, S. 126
mnemonics 37, 39, 77, 119, 132, 134
mock exams 7-8, 34, 82
Moonwalking with Einstein (Foer, 2011)
Morris, L. 4
motivational theory 2
multiple-choice questions 75, 131
mushrooms, facts about 92-3

National Professional Qualification for Headship (NPQH) 67, 139
National Professional Qualification for Senior Leadership (NPQSL) 67, 139
negative self-belief 2, 4
neural plasticity 68, 72; *see also* brain plasticity
new theory of disuse 33, 38-40, 39, 106, 108, 111-12, 122

Nitty Gritty boxes *xiii*, 7, 16, 143-4; desirable difficulties 35-6, 38, 42, 46-7; fear appeals 25, 29, 30 giving back control 81; intervention 73, 76; metacognition of learning 117, 119-20, 122
Noyes, A. 127
Nutshell boxes *xiii*; desirable difficulties 37-8, 49; dream for education 126-7; fear appeals 24; intervention 72, 74-5; metacognition of learning 118, 120-1; self-efficacy 60, 64, 68

off-task behaviours 11-12
optimal testing schedules 48; worked examples 51-2, **52**

pandemic *see* Covid-19 pandemic
parent engagement *xiv*, 141
parent lead 141
parental expectations 8
parents' evenings/events 8-11, 18, 141
pastoral lead 140; suggestions for 17-19
pastoral management 138
pastoral roles 15
PASTORAL Scheme of Work *see* Personal, Social, Health and Economic (PSHE)
pastoral support **44**
PEEL (Point, Evidence, Explanation, Link) 8
peer evaluation 117
peer interaction 10
perceived control 6, 64; definition 1, 58, 61-2, *62*
perceptual motor skills 42, 116
perfectionism 8
performance: anxiety 72-3; data 14-15; management 138
Personal, Social, Health and Economic (PSHE) *xii, xiv*, 80, 82-4, 128-9, 140-3; defining test anxiety 2, 5, 7-14, 16-19; desirable difficulties 33, 38, 40, 43-4, 47, 49, 53-4; fear appeals 24-6, 28, 30-1; intervention 71, 73-7, 86-7, 94, 114; metacognition of learning 120-2; school development plans 138; self-efficacy 59-60, 64-5
Pescod, M. 62
physical space 23
physics **52**
positive affirmation 16-17
positive messages 71, 76
positive test representatives 87-8
PowerPoint presentations 108, 128, 142
practice sessions 132
primary/KS2 (10-11-year-olds) 83, **87**, 88-93
priming anxiety 13, 82; definition 80

prose passages: meta-memory of 42, 109, 116
proximal anxiety 3-4
proximal factors 2-3
psychology 89, 95
Putwain, D. 3, 6, 10, 24, 61-3, 72, 108

questionnaires 82; benefits of 11; self-efficacy 59-60; *see also* Children's Test Anxiety Questionnaire (CTAS); Children's Test Attitude Questionnaires
Quintilian 68-9
quizzes 50-1

Ramirez, G. 75, 108
re-reading 37, 42, 49, 90-2, 95, 101, 109, 132
reading 5
recall aids recall 68, 71, 74, 81, 87, 116, 119, 139, 143; definition 71, 80
recall periods 15, 44, **44**, 50, 134, 141
relationships: student-teacher 71, 75
religious education 139
retention: definition 97
retrieval fluency 115, 118-20, 122-3, 132
retrieval practice *xiii, xiv*, 29, 69, 130, 133, 139; benefits of 135; defining test anxiety 15-16; desirable difficulties 33-4, 41, 45-7, 53; intervention 73-4, 95, 109; metacognition of learning 118, 122
retrieval strength 111
revision: habits *xii*; materials 50; methods 37; notes 49; optimal schedules *xiv*, 51-2; skills *xiv*
revolutionary plans 16
Robinson, K. 23, 126
Roediger, H. 31, 40-2, 53, 95, 97-8, 109, 116

SATs (Statutory Assessment Tests) 1-2, 23
SCAMPER technique 125-7
Scheme of Work *see* Personal, Social, Health and Economic (PSHE)
school development plans *xii, xiv*, 53-4, 62, 65, 122, 127, 138-42; activities and stages **139-41**; defining test anxiety 8, 15-16, 18; fear appeals 28, 30-1; feedback 139, **139-41**; intervention 80, 82
school refusal 65
school, terminology *xiii*
science learning 43
secondary/KS3 (11-14-year-olds) 83, **94**, 95-102
secondary/KS4 (14-16-year-olds) 83, **103**, 104-5
secondary/KS5 (16-18+ year olds) 83-4, **108**, 109, 111-13
self-belief 6

self-efficacy *xii*, 5, 34, 58-69, 72, 80, 121-2; definition 1; 'problem to solution and outcome' model 64; questionnaire 59-60; scenarios 65-7; strategies 64-5; theory *xiii*, xiv, 6, 58-9, 67, 73, 81
self-esteem 26, 72
self-knowledge beliefs 2, *3*, *4*, 59; definition 1
Self-Referent Executive Function (S-REF) Model 2, *3*, *4*, 59, 61, 73
self-reflection **44**
SENCOs *see* Special Educational Needs Co-ordinators (SENCOs)
SEND *see* special educational needs and disabilities (SEND)
senior management team (SMT) agenda 65, 138, 140
Shanks, D. R. 29
Shea, J. 118
short answer recall 135
sickness 63
silence in examinations 5, 144
Simonides of Ceos 68
skills deficits 2
Smith, R. J. 61
Snapchat 17
snowflake generation 11, 42
soapbox *xiii*, *xiv*, 15; desirable difficulties 46, 54; fear appeals 23, 25; metacognition of learning 117-19, 121; school development plans 138; self-efficacy 63; *see also* dream for education
social experiments 29
social media 10, 17, 50-1, 76
spacing 36-7, 49, **52**, 94, 103, 108-9, 117, 139; definition 100, 115; study 132
Spanish 39, 40
Special Educational Needs Co-ordinators (SENCOs) 9, 13-14, 26, 65-7
special educational needs and disabilities (SEND) 66; newsletters 66; policy 66
Speller scheme 46
spelling: interleaved system 46; rocks 32, 34; tests 45-7; teaching strategies 133
Spielberger, C. D. 3
SREF *see* Self-Referent Executive Function (S-REF) Model
stability bias 121-2; definition 106, 121
staff training *see* training
'star' awards 45
state and trait anxiety: contextual exam anxiety 7; definition of 1
state anxiety 7, 20, 61-2
statistics 3
storage strength 111
stranger danger 61
student-teacher relationships 71, 75

study periods 15, **44**; *see also* recall periods
study rooms 34, 100-1
'study, test, test, test' model *xiii*, 27, 133, 140-1, 143; defining test anxiety 15-16, 18; desirable difficulties 38, 48-9, 51, 53; intervention 77, 87, 89, 91, 94, 96, 102, 104; metacognition of learning 116, 118
Sumeracki, M. 29
summarization 37, 132
Symes, W. 6

Teacher Toolkit 29
Teacher Training 63; on Desirable Difficulties *xii*; materials **44**; Programme 128; Standards 118
teacher-student relationships 71
teachers, suggestions for 66
Teaching Assistants (TAs) 19
Teaching Standards 20, 130; Teaching Standard '2/8' 139
test anxiety *xii*, *xiv*; benefits of 3; definition *xiv*, 1-20; history of 2-3; intervening in *see* intervention; managing 2; measurement of 13; models of 2, 4; parents and students 8; problem of 80; reducing 80-113; scenarios 17-19; supporting 14-16; theory *xiii*, 2, 81
testing diary **44**
testing effect 64, 122, 130-1, 133; benefits of 73-4; best times to test 40-1; defining test anxiety 16; definition of 33; desirable difficulties 34, 37, 44, **44**, **52**, 53; intervention 72-4, 80-1, 85, 94-5, 103, 108-9
tests: definition *xiii*
Themistocles 69
Theodectes 69
thoughts 11
timetables 119
timing of tests 48
training 63; attributional 14-15, 19, 138, 141
trait anxiety 3, 7, 20, 25-6, 61-2
transactional: definition 1; model 4

uncertain control 64; definition 58, 61-2, *62*
United Kingdom (UK): Initial Teacher Training framework 127
United States (US) 29
unknown content 41
using tests: definition 100

Vagg, P. R. 3
VAK (visual, audio and kinesthetic) 131
varying conditions of practice 131; context 100
verbal-conceptual procedural skills 42, 116

Weems, C. F. 13, 60, 63, 73
wellbeing 60, 65-7, 73, 75, 81, 121; definition 58; negative effect on 62-3; retrieval practice for *xiii*; strategies *xiii*
WhatsApp 16-17
Whitten, W. B. 48
whole-school development plans 116
why: definition 71
working memory *see* low-working memory; memory
worry/worrying 2; concept of 4; definition of 1
Wren, D. 11

Yan, V. X. 117
Yang, C. 29, 53
Yates, G. 109, 118
Yeager, D. S. 75
year groups 82
Yen Mar, A.: *Chinese Cinderella* 5
younger students 115, 122

Zeidner, M. 2-4, 58, 61
Zhao, W. 29

For Product Safety Concerns and Information please contact our EU
representative GPSR@taylorandfrancis.com
Taylor & Francis Verlag GmbH, Kaufingerstraße 24, 80331 München, Germany

www.ingramcontent.com/pod-product-compliance
Lightning Source LLC
Chambersburg PA
CBHW082101230426
43670CB00017B/2911